A BRIGHTER SHADE OF BLACK

Why The World's Poorest Continent Isn't As Poor As You Think

Dr. Mwenya Kasonde

Sishima Publishing

Co. Cavan, Ireland.

First published in Republic of Ireland 2015

Copyright © Sishima Publishing

The right of Mwenya Kasonde to be identified as Author has been asserted in accordance with the Copyright, Design and Patents Act 1988.

ISBN 978-0-9934403-1-1

All rights reserved; no part of this publication may be reproduced, stored in a retrieval system, or transmitted in any form or by any means, electronic or mechanical, photocopying, recording, or otherwise without the prior written permission of the Publisher. This book may not be lent, resold, hired out or otherwise disposed of by way of trade in any form of binding or cover other than that in which it is published without the prior written consent of the Publisher.

To my father, Dr. Joseph M. Kasonde and my mother, Mrs Mary C. Kasonde, the two brightest people I know.

A Brighter Shade of Black

Mwenya Kasonde

Table of Contents

Introduction

Chapter 1.   Africa the Great

Chapter 2.   The Big Lie

Chapter 3.   Lifestyle Leaders

Chapter 4.   Business and Finance

Chapter 5.   Peace and Democracy

Chapter 6.   High-Tech Revolution

Chapter 7.   The Changing Face

Chapter 8.   Health and Education

Chapter 9.   Land of Opportunity

Foreword

The impetus to write this book came from watching a BBC TV documentary. As the program progressed my sister and I became increasingly frustrated and angry. The subject was about immigrants to the UK from Africa and the Caribbean and what a splendid contribution we were making to the nation.

The focus was on people working as bus conductors and traffic wardens and in other service industry roles. There was no mention whatsoever of the university graduates who were working in the city or as doctors in hospitals!

This was the final straw. I had already become aggravated by the Western media's portrayal of my home continent of Africa. I was less than impressed by the self-serving celebrity do-gooders who wanted to save the continent from itself and—as they sought to raise funds—perpetuated the stereotype of a continent that was a bleak, hopeless place: the "dark continent." As if, in the 21st century, as back in the 19th century, Westerners felt compelled to come to the rescue.

I know a different Africa. A continent that is becoming a powerful force in the world. A continent no longer torn apart like it once was by horrific civil wars, famine and abject poverty. A continent with peace and democracy…dramatically improving economies….enhanced education and healthcare…amazing developments in infrastructure.

Africa is the continent of the 21st century. And that's a story that needs to be told. Of course, serious problems and challenges endure. To ignore or deny them would only undermine my credibility. I am not an undiscerning Pollyanna who sugar coats reality.

But despite great strides forward, the continent continues to be marginalized and it has yet to claim its rightful spot on the world stage.

It's time to hear about the new Africa. And that is why I needed to write this book. I hope to play a small role in opening eyes to the boundless possibilities that exist in this great continent. It is a story about the exciting, emerging Africa that I like to think of as A Brighter Shade of Black.

Introduction.

"The darkest thing about Africa has always been our ignorance of it."

--GEORGE KIMBLE, HISTORIAN

War. Poverty. AIDS. Famine. Disease. Corruption.

These are the words that probably spring to mind when most people in the western world think of Africa.

It's still the "dark continent"—a term coined in 1878 by British journalist and explorer Henry Stanley in a book about his travels. A few years earlier, Stanley had gained fame by tracking down the 'missing' missionary Dr. David Livingstone, greeting him with the historic words, "Dr. Livingstone, I presume."

In the late 19th century Africa was largely unknown and little visited by Europeans. The phrase "dark continent" undoubtedly evoked a sense of mystery and adventure for the western reader. At the same time it expressed a sense of western superiority over African backwardness and, as Stanley saw it, the primitive lives of the "savages" he encountered.

Stanley wrote that, "the savage only respects force, power, boldness, and decision" and his legacy of death and destruction in the Congo region is considered an inspiration for Joseph Conrad's *Heart of Darkness*. But, generally, Stanley is still remembered and lionized in the west as a heroic figure while the stereotype of Africa as the "dark continent" persists.

In the late 19th century the European powers held a widespread belief that they had a duty to civilize the peoples they had colonized. While there are different interpretations of Rudyard Kipling's famous poem in which he wrote (not specifically of Africa) of the "white man's burden" it cannot be denied that the poem epitomized the prevailing paternalistic attitude.

"Take up the White Man's burden--

Send forth the best ye breed--

Go bind your sons to exile

To serve your captives' need;

To wait in heavy harness,

On fluttered folk and wild--

Your new-caught, sullen peoples,

Half-devil and half-child."

"Dark continent." "Half-devil and half-child."

These are the colorful creative writings and portrayals of the 1880s and 1890s that have hung over the image of Africa even until today. There is no escaping the fact that the continent has endured decades of war and genocide; millions have lost their lives through disease and famine; corrupt politicians have brought fledgling nations to their knees; and natural and man-made disasters of one kind or another have ravaged country after country.

AFRICA ON THE RISE

But the Africa of the 21st century is an entirely different matter. It is a continent that is on the rise—and from every perspective. Let's first examine and quantify some of the key areas in which dramatic progress is being made.

Financial and Economic:

- The International Monetary Fund forecasts that Africa will have the fastest-growing economy of any continent over the next five years. Already it boasts six of the 10 fastest-growing countries in the world with an average growth rate of over five percent.

- Over the past 10 years real income per person has improved by upwards of 30 percent—a dramatic change from the previous 20 years when it declined by nearly 10 percent.

- Foreign direct investment has stepped up from $15 billion in 2002 to $46 billion in 2012.

- About 60 percent of the world's uncultivated arable land is in Africa, according to the McKinsey Global Institute.

- More than 20 sub-Saharan countries, with more than 400 million people, have gained middle-income status, reports the World Bank.

Health and Education:

- Malaria deaths in some of the worst-hit countries have dropped by 30 percent in the past decade.

- HIV infections have decreased by as much as 74 percent.

- Life expectancy across the continent has risen by about 10 percent while child mortality rates have dropped sharply.

- Secondary-school enrolment grew by 48 percent between 2000 and 2008 as a result of a concerted effort by many states and the elimination of school fees.

Lifestyle:

- Mobile phones are everywhere. There are currently three mobile phones for every four people, the same as India. With 500 million subscribers Africa is on its way to becoming the world leader in the use of mobile technology.

- Television sets are expected to have a place in 30 percent of homes by 2017, a fivefold increase over 10 years.

- Movie-making is no longer ruled by Hollywood or Bollywood. Nigeria alone produces more movies than America.

In March 2013, in a major article titled "Africa Rising," *The Economist* magazine commented, "…the numbers suggest that human development in sub-Saharan Africa has made huge leaps."

It went on, "Today Africa is the continent of the future—a vast landscape of youthfulness, enterprise and resources on the verge of exercising its potential." And also, "Film-makers, novelists, designers, musicians and artists thrive in a new climate of hope."

HOPE AND GROWTH

Africa is, indeed, a continent of hope, especially if the opinion polls are to be believed. Africans by and large are optimistic about the future. Almost two-thirds say that this year will be better than last—double the number of Europeans who feel the same way.

Africa is also a continent of growth, in every way imaginable.

- Africa has the youngest population of any continent with almost 200 million aged between 15 and 24—a number expected to double by 2045.

- It is projected that by 2040 the total African population will be the largest in the world, surpassing both China and India.

United Nations predictions are that overall population will quadruple over 90 years "an astonishingly rapid growth," says *The Economist*, "that will make Africa more important than ever." The magazine adds, "And it's not just that there will be four times the workforce, four times the resource burden, four times as many voters. The rapid growth itself will likely transform political and social dynamics within African countries and thus their relationship with the rest of the world."

So much for the numbers for now. I use them at this point as an overall indicator that Africa is no longer the continent that you might think it is. In this book I will illustrate just as graphically with stories—stories of people and their endeavors. It can only be a selection of stories, but stories that are nevertheless representative of the new Africa.

I am a huge admirer of the renowned Nigerian writer Chimamanda Adichie. This is a quote from her that particularly resonates with me.

> **"Stories have been used to dispossess and to malign but stories can also be used to empower and to humanize. Stories can break the dignity of a people but stories can also repair that broken dignity."**

In July 2009 Adichie stood in front of a rapt audience in Oxford, England and delivered a TED talk in which she spoke of the "single story" and more specifically of the "danger of the single story."

Adichie shows that stories play an integral part of our lives, constantly shaping our views of the world and of each other. Adichie shares a personal tale of a domestic worker that was employed by her parents. Adichie's mother constantly tells the children that this boy's family is poor. When the children do not finish their dinner, their mother admonishes them, urging them to eat and be grateful because, unlike their house boy, they have food and are not poor.

It is only when Adichie visits the boy's family that she realizes that the sum of all of these individual comments have added up to a story of the boy's family, one with a defining theme of poverty. During the visit, she is surprised to see some beautiful baskets created by one family member. Adichie had only thought of them as poor. She had not even considered them to be artistic or capable or rich in any way.

This story is an example of a single story that focuses only on one aspect of someone's life or existence to the exclusion of all others. As Chimamanda Adichie says, "That is how to create a single story. Show a people as one thing, as only one thing over and over again and that is what they become." The main character of a single story is often dehumanized and becomes the subject of pity. The person creating the single story has the power to limit the other, painting the personality of the protagonists in broad brushstrokes and enforcing the limitations of helplessness at best and stupidity or savagery at worst.

Adichie contends (and in writing this book I obviously agree) that there has been a single story of the African continent as portrayed elsewhere and particularly in the west. To illustrate this point, she talks about coming to the United States as a college student and meeting her roommate. The roommate is surprised that Adichie is not dirt poor, that she speaks English, and that she even owns Mariah Carey CDs. This roommate had a single story of Africans as poor and incapable people to be pitied and helped. It is important to understand that the roommate did not come to this conclusion by herself. She did not independently conjure up the plot points and characterizations that led to a single and limiting story.

Instead, she formed this viewpoint from overheard conversations, from books, movies, and newspapers. The fact is that portrayals of Africa in popular culture and the news media typically paint a bleak picture of the continent. Take a look at any American newspaper, for example, and see what it says about Africa. As I mentioned at the beginning of the chapter I am quite sure that most stories focus on war, poverty, AIDS, famine, disease and corruption.

Hollywood films that portray Africa are no better often leaving Western audiences with the impression that the continent is nothing more than a hotbed for conflict (as in *Blood Diamond*). Alternatively, the continent is seen through the lens of a Western narrator or main character—*Out of Africa* and *The Last King of Scotland* being prime examples.

It is disturbing, that an entire continent can continue to be defined through a single story.

Chimamanda Adichie is from Nigeria, only one of the 54 countries that comprise the African continent. And yet, while in the United States, she is expected to speak for Africa as a whole, from the tip of South Africa to Kenya to Senegal and everywhere in between, an area that takes up 11,668,598.7 square miles (or 30,221,532 square kilometers). It is only when she travels to the U.S. and is asked to speak as an African that Adichie discovers an African identity that she did not even know existed.

That's the West's single story of Africa and it is also one that minimizes its own role in the negative issues that have plagued the continent. Of course, Western countries have spread their largesse throughout Africa with aid packages of one kind or another. But the benefits of some of those programs are also up for debate.

There are those who argue that aid to Africa must continue and even increase. Some Westerners still view the continent as a place that is in crisis and that will fall apart without their hand-outs. Others counter that an ongoing campaign for aid only serves to highlight the financial ties that bind Africa to her former colonial masters and that Africa should and can become self-sufficient. As we will see the emerging Africa is beginning to stand on its own feet.

WHAT BONO DOESN'T SAY

I thoroughly agree with the views of William Easterly, esteemed professor of economics at New York University, Visiting Fellow at the Brookings Institution and the author of "The White Man's Burden: How the West's Efforts to Aid the Rest Have Done So Much Ill and So Little Good."

Back in July, 2007 he wrote an excellent article in the *Los Angeles Times* under the headline, "What Bono doesn't say about Africa; Celebrities like to portray it as a basket case, but they ignore very real progress."

I'd like to quote him directly because his words are so powerful:

"Just when it seemed that Western images of Africa could not get any weirder, the July

2007 special Africa issue of *Vanity Fair* was published, complete with a feature article on 'Madonna's Malawi.' At the same time, the memoirs of an African child soldier are on sale at your local Starbucks, and celebrity activist Bob Geldof is touring Africa yet again, followed by TV cameras, to document that 'War, Famine, Plague & Death are the Four Horsemen of the Apocalypse and these days they're riding hard through the back roads of Africa.'

"It's a dark and scary picture of a helpless, backward continent that's being offered up to TV watchers and coffee drinkers. But in fact, the real Africa is quite a bit different. And the problem with all this Western stereotyping is that it manages to snatch defeat from the jaws of some current victories, fueling support for patronizing Western policies designed to rescue the allegedly helpless African people while often discouraging those policies that might actually help."

Easterly goes on to challenge the stereotype pointing out that the percentage of the African population that dies in war every year, or the percentage of male kids aged 10 to 17 who are child soldiers, or the percentage of Africans suffering from famine or dying of aids or living as refugees is less than half of one percent, or much less.

"The typical African is a long way from being a starving, AIDS-stricken refugee at the mercy of child soldiers. The reality is that many more Africans need latrines than need Western peacekeepers—but that doesn't play so well on TV," says Easterly.

Easterly goes on to stress similar points to those I have already made and upon which I will later elaborate regarding dramatic improvement in economies and growth of living standards. And he poses the question: Why do aid organizations and their celebrity backers want to make African successes look like failures?

His answer: "One can only speculate, but it certainly helps aid agencies get more publicity and more money if problems seem greater than they are. As for the stars—well, could Africa be saving celebrity careers more than celebrities are saving Africa? In truth, Africans are and will be escaping poverty the same way everybody else did: through the efforts of resourceful entrepreneurs, democratic reformers and ordinary citizens at home, not through PR extravaganzas of ill-informed outsiders. The real Africa needs increased trade from the West more than it needs more aid handouts."

Easterly records how a respected Ugandan journalist, Andrew Mwenda, made this point at a recent African conference despite the fact that the world's most famous celebrity activist—Bono—was attempting to shout him down. Mwenda was suffering from too much reality for Bono's taste: "What man or nation has ever become rich by holding out a begging bowl?" asked Mwenda.

Writes Easterly, "Perhaps Bono was grouchy because his celebrity-laden 'Red' campaign to promote Western brands to finance begging bowls for Africa has spent $100 million on marketing and generated sales of only $18 million, according to a recent report."

He concluded, "Today, as I sip my Rwandan gourmet coffee and wear my Nigerian shirt here in New York, and as European men eat fresh Ghanaian pineapple for breakfast and bring Kenyan flowers home to their wives, I wonder what it will take for Western consumers to learn even more about the products of self-sufficient, hardworking, dignified Africans. Perhaps they should spend less time consuming Africa disaster stereotypes from television and *Vanity Fair*."

THE AFRICAN TIGER

The same theme was pursued by *New York Times* columnist, Pulitzer Prize-winner, and Africa expert, Nicholas Kristof, in a June 2012 column: "Generations of Americans have learned to pity Africa. It's mainly seen as a quagmire of famine and genocide, a destination only for a sybaritic safari or a masochistic aid mission. So here's another way to think of Africa: an economic dynamo."

Citing similar statistics to those I mentioned earlier in this chapter Kristof went on, "Is it time to prepare for the African tiger economy? Africa isn't just a place for safaris or humanitarian aid. It's also a place to make money. Global companies are expanding in Africa; vast deposits of oil, gas and minerals are being discovered; and Goldman Sachs recently issued a report, "Africa's Turn," comparing business opportunities in Africa with those in China in the early 1990s...I'm a strong supporter of foreign aid, but economic growth and job creation are ultimately the most sustainable way to raise living standards. All in all, though, Africa is becoming more democratic, more technocratic and more market-friendly. Yet many Westerners are largely oblivious to the idea of Africa as a success story.

"One of the problems with journalism is that we focus on disasters. We cover planes that crash, not those that take off. In Africa, that means we cover famine in Somalia and genocide in Sudan, terrorism in Nigeria and warlords in Congo. Those are important stories—deserving more attention, not less—but they can also leave a casual reader convinced that all of Africa is lurching between genocide and famine."

Kristof was writing his column from Lesotho, a country that had just had a democratic change of power. He ended by writing, "Its streets are safe, and it is working on becoming one of the first countries in the world with an electric grid 100 percent reliant on renewable energy. It's a symbol of an Africa that is rising."

So, in this book I am going to relate the stories of resilient people who are part of the Africa that is rising, who refuse to be pigeonholed by the common perceptions of Africa. These are people who see Africa as a place of growth and progress instead of an epicenter of stagnation and decay. These people and their efforts to build a brighter future underscore the breadth and diversity of the continent. Africa is not the monolithic entity that American television viewers would believe. Instead it is a vibrant and evolving organism pulsating with new ideas and energy waiting to be released.

The individuals, communities and companies profiled in this book are taking the first step toward bringing Africa out of the darkness that many years of misunderstanding and negative portrayals have created.

Chapter 1. Africa the Great

It gives one hope, this great strength of Africa.

—STEPHEN LEWIS, FORMER CANADIAN AMBASSADOR TO THE UNITED NATIONS - UN SPECIAL ENVOY FOR HIV/AIDS IN AFRICA

Self-made billionaires. International fashion designers. Peace and democracy. Gleaming skyscraper cities. High-speed rail. Mobile technology pioneers.

This is the picture of the emerging Africa that you will find in the pages of this book. Not war, poverty, AIDS, famine, disease and corruption - words which have been overused and are well past us.

There are billionaires who have made their fortunes through spearheading the mobile revolution. More SIM cards are already being used in Africa than in North America—and the staggering rate of growth continues. There are billionaires who have capitalized on the increasing development of the continent's infrastructure through their cement and oil businesses. There are billionaires who have pursued mining opportunities and the remarkable expansion of telecommunications. These are the people I want to introduce you to.

Africa is emerging as a style leader and trendsetter in fashion, music, arts, entertainment, and writing. Sons and daughters of the continent, influenced by its great traditions are spreading the word throughout the world and some, who have become part of the diaspora, are returning home to influence their countrymen to take charge of their own futures rather than rely on foreign aid.

The theme of self-reliance rather than dependence on charitable aid is one that you will find woven throughout these pages as I am less than impressed by the self-serving celebrity do-gooders who, while seeking to raise funds, have perpetuated the stereotype of a continent that is still a bleak, hopeless place: the "dark continent." The Western media has been complicit in fostering the image and the need for the continent to be "rescued" as if we were still living in the 1800s.

Africa is not a continent just comprised of jungles and deserts. Today glistening skyscraper cities are being built from scratch in many countries. I will give you examples from Kenya to Ghana; from the Democratic Republic of Congo (DRC) to Rwanda. Africa is going to have the biggest and the best in many ways. The biggest dam in the world—in the DRC.

The world's biggest investment in renewable energy—in South Africa. One of the world's biggest deep space telescopes—also in South Africa.

It is a continent of superlatives. A continent of extremes.

It is the oldest and the youngest. The continent that was the birthplace of mankind now has a younger population than anywhere else on the planet with 65 percent of its people under the age of 25.

It is the world's second largest continent, embracing all four hemispheres and inhabited by more than a billion people.

There are about 2,000 different languages spoken throughout Africa. Its unique history of migration and colonization has created one of the most diverse and yet convergent societies in the world.

It is home to more than a quarter of the countries of the world.

It has jungles. It has deserts. It has dramatic coastlines. It even has a glacier.

AFRICA ON THE RISE

The Africa of the 21st century is a continent that is on the rise—and from every perspective. Let's first examine and quantify some of the key areas in which dramatic progress is being made.

Financial and Economic:

▪ The International Monetary Fund forecasts that Africa will have the fastest-growing economy of any continent over the next five years. Already it boasts six of the 10 fastest-growing countries in the world with an average growth rate of over five percent.

▪ Over the past 10 years real income per person has improved by upwards of 30 percent—a dramatic change from the previous 20 years when it declined by nearly 10 percent.

- Foreign direct investment has stepped up from $15 billion in 2002 to $46 billion in 2012. This gives people the opportunity to prove themselves instead of accepting hand-outs.

- About 60 percent of the world's uncultivated arable land is in Africa, according to the McKinsey Global Institute.

- More than 20 sub-Saharan countries, with more than 400 million people, have gained middle-income status, reports the World Bank.

Health and Education:

- Malaria deaths in some of the worst-hit countries have dropped by 30 percent in the past decade.

- HIV infections have decreased by as much as 74 percent in some places.

- Life expectancy across the continent has risen by about 10 percent while child mortality rates have dropped sharply.

- Secondary-school enrolment grew by 48 percent between 2000 and 2008 as a result of a concerted effort by many states and the elimination of school fees.

Lifestyle

- Mobile phones are everywhere. There are currently three mobile phones for every four people, the same as India. With nearly 700 million subscribers Africa is on its way to becoming the world leader in the use of mobile technology. Africa has also spearheaded the use of digital and mobile payment technology in the past decade.

- Television sets are expected to have a place in 30 percent of homes by 2017, a fivefold increase over 10 years.

- Movie-making is no longer ruled by Hollywood or Bollywood. Nigeria alone produces more movies than America. And African fashion is challenging Paris, Milan and New York.

In March 2013, in a major article titled "Africa Rising," *The Economist* magazine commented, "…the numbers suggest that human development in sub-Saharan Africa has made huge leaps."

It went on, "Today Africa is the continent of the future—a vast landscape of youthfulness, enterprise and resources on the verge of exercising its potential." And also, "Film-makers, novelists, designers, musicians and artists thrive in a new climate of hope."

HOPE AND GROWTH

Africa is, indeed, a continent of hope, especially if the opinion polls are to be believed. Africans by and large are optimistic about the future. Almost two-thirds say that this year will be better than last—double the number of Europeans who feel the same way. This is wonderful transformation that may surprise, even shock, you. For, as we will discover in the next chapter, the perception of the continent is somewhat different and lags behind reality.

Chapter 2.   The Big Lie

Stories have been used to dispossess and to malign but stories can also be used to empower and to humanize. Stories can break the dignity of a people but stories can also repair that broken dignity.

-CHIMAMANDA ADICHIE

I am a huge admirer of the renowned Nigerian writer Chimamanda Adichie. This is a quote from her that particularly resonates with me. In July 2009 Adichie stood in front of a rapt audience in Oxford, England and delivered a TED talk in which she spoke of the "single story" and more specifically of the "danger of the single story."

Adichie shows that stories play an integral part of our lives, constantly shaping our views of the world and of each other. She shares a personal tale of a domestic worker that was employed by her parents. Adichie's mother constantly tells the children that this boy's family is poor. When the children do not finish their dinner, their mother admonishes them, urging them to eat and be grateful because, unlike their house boy, they have food and are not poor.

It is only when Adichie visits the boy's family that she realizes that the sum of all of these individual comments have added up to a story of the boy's family, one with a defining theme of poverty. During the visit, she is surprised to see some beautiful baskets created by one family member. She had only thought of them as poor! She had not even considered them to be artistic or capable or rich in any way.

This story is an example of a single story that focuses only on one aspect of someone's life or existence to the exclusion of all others. As Chimamanda Adichie says, "That is how to create a single story. Show a people as one thing, as only one thing over and over again and that is what they become." The main character of a single story is often dehumanized and becomes the subject of pity. The real tragedy however is when the African himself buys the story, and rests in fear and a feeling of hopelessness. The person creating the single story has the power to limit the other, painting the personality of the protagonists in broad brushstrokes and enforcing the limitations of helplessness at best and stupidity or savagery at worst.

Adichie contends, and I strongly agree, that there has been a single story of the African continent as portrayed in the West. To highlight this point, she talks about coming to the United States as a college student and meeting her roommate. The roommate is surprised that Adichie is not dirt poor, that she speaks English, and that she even owns Mariah Carey

CDs. This roommate had a single story of Africans as poor and incapable people to be pitied and helped. It is important to understand that the roommate did not come to this conclusion by herself. She did not independently conjure up the plot points and characterizations that led to a single and limiting story.

Instead, she formed this viewpoint from overheard conversations, from books, movies, and newspapers. The fact is that portrayals of Africa in popular culture and the news media typically paint a bleak picture of the continent. Take a look at the average Western newspaper, and see what it says about Africa. Most stories focus on war, poverty, AIDS, famine, disease and corruption.

Hollywood films that portray Africa leave Western audiences with the impression that the continent is nothing more than a hotbed for conflict (as in *Blood Diamond*). Alternatively, the continent is seen through the lens of a Western narrator or main character—*Out of Africa* and *The Last King of Scotland* being prime examples.

It is disturbing that an entire continent can continue to be defined through a single story.

Chimamanda Adichie is from Nigeria, only one of the 54 countries that comprise the African continent. And yet, while in the United States, she is expected to speak for Africa as a whole, from the tip of South Africa to Kenya to Senegal and everywhere in between, an area that takes up 11,668,598.7 square miles. It is only when she travels to the U.S. and is asked to speak as an African that Adichie discovers an African identity that she did not even know existed.

That's the West's single story of Africa and as the continent is so strongly influenced by western culture, some parts of this story have unfortunately crept into the minds of many Africans. Themselves believing that the only way is to beg your way out of poverty. Of course, Western countries have spread their largesse throughout Africa with aid packages of one kind or another. But the benefits of some of those programs are also up for debate.

There are those who argue that aid to Africa must continue and even increase. Some Westerners still view the continent as a place that is in crisis and that will fall apart without their hand-outs. Others counter that an ongoing campaign for aid only serves to highlight the financial ties that bind Africa to her former colonial masters and that Africa should and can become self-sufficient. Luckily, the emerging Africa is beginning to stand on its own feet.

WHAT BONO DOESN'T SAY

I thoroughly agree with the views of William Easterly, esteemed professor of economics at New York University and Visiting Fellow at the Brookings Institution. You can easily tell where he stands from the provocative title of his book The White Man's Burden: Why the West's Efforts to Aid the Rest Have Done So much Ill and so Little Good.

Back in July, 2007 he wrote an excellent article in the *Los Angeles Times* under the headline, "What Bono doesn't say about Africa; Celebrities like to portray it as a basket case, but they ignore very real progress."

I'd like to quote him directly because his words are so powerful:

"Just when it seemed that Western images of Africa could not get any weirder, the July 2007 special Africa issue of *Vanity Fair* was published, complete with a feature article on 'Madonna's Malawi.' At the same time, the memoirs of an African child soldier are on sale at your local Starbucks, and celebrity activist Bob Geldof is touring Africa yet again, followed by TV cameras, to document that 'War, Famine, Plague and Death are the Four Horsemen of the Apocalypse and these days they're riding hard through the back roads of Africa.'"

Adds Easterly, "It's a dark and scary picture of a helpless, backward continent that's being offered up to TV watchers and coffee drinkers. But, in fact, the real Africa is quite a bit different. And the problem with all this Western stereotyping is that it manages to snatch defeat from the jaws of some current victories, fueling support for patronizing Western policies designed to rescue the allegedly helpless African people while often discouraging those policies that might actually help."

Easterly goes on to challenge the stereotype pointing out that the percentage of the African population that dies in war every year, or the percentage of male kids aged 10 to 17 who are child soldiers, or the percentage of Africans suffering from famine or dying of aids or living as refugees, is less than half of one percent, or much less.

"The typical African is a long way from being a starving, AIDS-stricken refugee at the mercy of child soldiers. The reality is that many more Africans need latrines than need Western peacekeepers—but that doesn't play so well on TV," says Easterly.

Here, we are beginning to stress similar points and upon which I will elaborate regarding dramatic improvement in economies and growth of living standards. And he poses the question: Why do aid organizations and their celebrity backers want to make African successes look like failures?

His answer: "One can only speculate, but it certainly helps aid agencies get more publicity and more money if problems seem greater than they are. As for the stars—well, could Africa be saving celebrity careers more than celebrities are saving Africa? In truth, Africans are and will be escaping poverty the same way everybody else did: through the efforts of resourceful entrepreneurs, democratic reformers and ordinary citizens at home, not through PR extravaganzas of ill-informed outsiders. The real Africa needs increased trade from the West more than it needs more aid handouts." Trade not aid!

A respected Ugandan journalist, Andrew Mwenda, raised this issue at a recent African conference despite the fact that the world's most famous celebrity activist—Bono—was attempting to shout him down. Mwenda was suffering from too much reality for Bono's taste: "What man or nation has ever become rich by holding out a begging bowl?" asked Mwenda.

It is a well-known fact that Bono's celebrity-laden 'Red' campaign to promote Western brands to finance begging bowls for Africa has spent $100 million on marketing and generated sales of only $18 million, according to a recent report.

Easterly, writing elsewhere, laments that over five decades the West spent $2.3 trillion on foreign aid and still had not managed to get twelve-cent medicines to children to prevent half of all malaria deaths; four-dollar bed nets to poor families; or three dollars to each new mother to prevent five million child deaths.

DEAD AID

International economist Dr. Dambisa Moyo, author of the *New York Times* bestseller *Dead Aid: Why Aid is Not Working and How There is a Better Way for Africa* is firmly in the same school of thought as Easterly. She doesn't mice her words, saying, "Aid is an unmitigated political, economic and humanitarian disaster."

She uses expression such as "rampant corruption" and "bloated bureaucracies" and maintains that aid is a "debilitating drug" that countries have a hard time weaning themselves off. "A constant stream of 'free' money is a perfect way to keep an inefficient or simply bad government in power," she says.

Zambian-born Moyo, named by *TIME Magazine* as one of the "100 Most Influential People in the World," contends that aid creates rather than solves challenges in the developing world. She calculates that over a 60-year period more than $1 trillion in development-related aid transferred from rich countries to Africa has in many ways had a detrimental effect.

She compares countries that have rejected aid and prospered with those who have become permanently aid-dependent, trapped in a vicious cycle of aid dependency, corruption, market distortion and further poverty.

Says Moyo, who is also a member of the World Economic Forum's Young Global Leaders Forum, "Giving alms to Africa remains one of the biggest ideas of our time—millions march for it, governments are judged by it, celebrities proselytize the need for it. Calls for more aid to Africa are growing louder, with advocates pushing for doubling the roughly $50 billion of international assistance that already goes to Africa each year.

"Yet evidence overwhelmingly demonstrates that aid to Africa has made the poor poorer, and the growth slower. The insidious aid culture has left African countries more debt-laden, more inflation-prone, more vulnerable to the vagaries of the currency markets and more unattractive to higher-quality investment. It's increased the risk of civil conflict and unrest."

FEEL GOOD

The fact remains that no country has ever grown rich by being given aid. Countries grow rich as a results of open markets. Aid only makes the giver feel good about himself and believe that he or she has in giving, secured a place in heaven.

Thanks to a crack in the European Union regulations Kenyan flower growers seized the opportunity to expand. It's now the biggest industry in the country and exports flowers as far as Amsterdam.

THE AFRICAN TIGER

The same theme was pursued by *New York Times* columnist, Pulitzer Prize-winner, and Africa expert, Nicholas Kristof, in a June 2012 column: "Generations of Americans have learned to pity Africa. It's mainly seen as a quagmire of famine and genocide, a destination only for a sybaritic safari or a masochistic aid mission. So here's another way to think of Africa: an economic dynamo."

Citing similar statistics to those I mentioned earlier in this chapter Kristof went on, "Is it time to prepare for the African tiger economy? Africa isn't just a place for safaris or humanitarian aid. It's also a place to make money. Global companies are expanding in Africa; vast deposits of oil, gas and minerals are being discovered; and Goldman Sachs recently issued a report, "Africa's Turn," comparing business opportunities in Africa with those in China in the early 1990s...I'm a strong supporter of foreign aid, but economic growth and jobs are ultimately the most sustainable way to raise living standards. All in all, though, Africa is becoming more democratic, more technocratic and more market-friendly. Yet Americans are largely oblivious to the idea of Africa as a success story."

One of the problems with journalism said Kristof is its focus on disasters. The media covers planes that crash, not those that take off. In Africa, that means covering famine in Somalia and genocide in Sudan, terrorism in Nigeria and warlords in Congo. Unfortunately for Africans and the world alike; bad news sells better than good news.

Newspapers may choose to report only the negative but that should not be our focus nor indeed the only information available about Africa.

Kristof was writing his column from Lesotho, a country that had just had a democratic change of power. He ended by writing, "Its streets are safe, and it is working on becoming one of the first countries in the world with an electric grid 100 percent reliant on renewable energy. It's a symbol of an Africa that is rising."

I plan to continue on this legacy and with this book relate the stories of resilience that is part of the Africa that is rising. There are people who refuse to be pigeonholed by the common perceptions of Africa. These are people who see Africa as a place of growth and progress instead of an epicenter of stagnation and decay. These people and their efforts to build a brighter future underscore the breadth and diversity of the continent. Africa is not the monolithic entity that Western television viewers would believe. Instead it is a vibrant and evolving organism pulsating with new ideas and energy waiting to be released.

Chapter 3. Lifestyle Leaders

History will show that Africa gave more than it ever received. It is the true donor nation.

–OZWALD BOATENG

The rhythm of life in Africa has given rise to an inspiring group of pioneers in the worlds of art and entertainment. From creative fashion designers to masterful musicians, from award-winning actors to influential novelists…it's remarkable how much talent has emerged from the continent.

And, by and large, many of these unique individuals are not satisfied with their success in their chosen endeavors, they are also working to give back to Africa and are encouraging both African self-sufficiency and for members of the diaspora to contribute.

Let's begin with the world of fashion and Ozwald Boateng. He is not just a world-renowned fashion icon—he's also a true champion for Africa. His "Made in Africa

Foundation" is focused on raising hundreds of millions of dollars to help build the continent's infrastructure.

While wearing an Ozwald Boateng suit turns you into a "statesman of cool" according to actor Laurence Fishbourne, the U.S. broadcaster National Public Radio (NPR), goes much further, saying "He's also a statesman for something else, the future development of Africa."

Boateng, born in London of Ghanaian parents, promotes the view that there is a new "wind of change" blowing through the continent. Fifty years ago it was political change—independence of nations. Today it is economic change—with the people of African nations gaining financial independence through their own actions and not from the dictates of colonial powers. The change, will be just as permanent and just as shocking.

Boateng somewhat colorfully says, "this change will not happen because of a million posters showing our babies starving with flies in their eyes or the perpetual funds raised for mosquito nets as a panacea against our ineffective drainage systems, though the lives of many were saved by campaigns such as these. It will come as our Tunisian Spring, a revolution sprung by social media, and as insistent as the ringtone of our mobile phones."

Boateng is a great believer in members of the African diaspora making their contribution to the growth of the continent. In June of 2013 his foundation made an impact at the 50th anniversary meeting of the African Development Bank (AfDB) bringing celebrities such as John Legend, Mos Def, Isaiah Washington, Youssou N'Dour and Akon to support the bank's audacious $68 billion plan to transform the continent in building railways, roads, clean water supplies—basic infrastructure that people in the West take for granted. The AfDB's plan, is to raise funds through a guarantee backed by the African nations: Africa helping Africans—the ultimate trade-not-aid policy.

HARMONY IN CONTRASTS

Describing his role he says, "I mixed these great talents from the diaspora and Africa in amongst the finance ministers, bankers and entrepreneurs. This is what a designer looks for: the harmony in contrasts. They find their common desire to make it happen—one group bringing this solution to the global audience, giving it transparency and encouraging investment, and the other group implementing it."

Boateng has traveled a long way since his early upbringing in the Muswell Hill district of London when he seemed destined to become a style leader, although no-one would have guessed his emergence as a "statesman." His mother had his first bespoke suit made for him when he was just five years old. His father was a teacher, and wore suits to school every day and the family always dressed well to go to church. This is how he became accustomed to a sense of style. He recalled later, "It was almost a way of life in my household to look good."

At age 14, Boateng found a summer job sewing linings into suits. At age 16, he was studying computer science when his girlfriend introduced him to cutting and designing, and this turned out to be his true vocation. He started designing clothes and selling them to fellow students and switched from computer science to a fashion and design course. After helping a friend make clothes for a fashion show and receiving high praise he did his own thing and soon sold his first collection to a menswear shop in Covent Garden.

Success followed success. In 1994, Boateng became the first tailor to present a catwalk show during Paris Fashion Week. Mentored by Tommy Nutter, the following year he opened his own boutique near the south end of Savile Row, the London street famed for its fine tailoring. In 2002 he became the youngest and first black tailor to have a store on Savile Row itself. Later, Boateng was honored with a major 20-year retrospective at the Victoria and Albert Museum and in 2008 his new flagship store and headquarters were launched at 30 Savile Row. British-Ghanaian architect David Adjaye co-designed the signage and interiors.

INFRASTRUCTURE ADVOCATE

But how did Boateng get from his humble beginning in London to achieving international recognition of his trademark twist on classic British tailoring and then becoming a passionate advocate for building Africa's infrastructure? He says it's quite simple. He just wanted to open shops "back home." But when he investigated what was required it took him into the wider world of master planning and infrastructure.

"If you don't have the infrastructure or the refinery to refine your own natural resources, then you're never getting true value for the value of your asset," he says, pointing out that Africa controls 60 percent of all the known minerals on the planet.

He says his foundation identified the fact that a key problem to unlocking the continent's potential was the perpetual difficulty in finding someone willing to take the risk of putting the first dollar into the feasibility plan for any infrastructure project, whether urban development, road or rail. So the foundation's objective is to "finance that first dollar."

To this end it is seeking to raise $400 million which he says will create a hundred billion dollars of projects across the continent and effectively create about a trillion dollars of value. What that also does, he maintains, is add another 2 percent of GDP on the continent and get another 200 million people out of poverty.

MADE IN GHANA

Boateng is not the only British-Ghanaian fashion designer enjoying international attention. Abenaa Pokuaa is the creator of the Ohema Ohene brand. In the Ghanaian language of Twi it means Queen and King and Pokuaa named it in homage both to her Ghanaian heritage and the fact that she creates clothing for women and men.

Pokuaa got her fashion degree at London College of Fashion. Her brand, which evolved after a spell working in the Far East and from a trip to Ghana, blends quintessentially British styling with West African textiles. Ohema Ohene says their fashion-forward, high-quality products gives the wearer a sense of style and glamour, representative of London's multicultural population.

Many of the rich prints Pokuaa uses are directly sourced from Ghana, blending authentic traditional motifs with more contemporary imagery. In addition, she also designs many of the prints herself utilizing Dutch Wax prints from Holland. The majority of the company's products are made in Ghana delivering a valuable source of trade for its people and in April 2013 Ohema Ohene set up a workshop in Accra, the country's capital, where it trains and employs Ghanaians to produce its products.

INDEPENDENT DESIGN

Another fashion designer working hard to put Africa at the forefront is Thula Sindi, one of South Africa's leading young stars. His eponymous self-titled clothing label features delicately-crafted women's wear.

Only 28, Sindi is garnering a stream of accolades and awards. Named by *Forbes* magazine in February 2013 as one of Africa's best young entrepreneurs, he was also the South African Small Enterprise Development Agency's Best Youth Entrepreneur of 2012, and SA Tourism's South African Designer of the Year for 2012.

After finishing his studies at the London International School of Fashion he became head designer at the Dutch firm Vlisco, but it wasn't long before he branched out to launch his own label.

Says Sindi, "My aim is to successfully build a large proudly African independent design enterprise, with beautiful, locally-manufactured merchandise. I want to prove that it is possible to have a designer-led business with ethical manufacturing practices, whilst creating a business model for other aspiring designers to follow in order to achieve commercial and creative success in the industry."

SOLE REBELS SINGULAR SUCCESS

Fashion extends to the tips of one's toes—and that's where a company called SoleRebels is pointing the way. Bethlehem Tilahun Alemu, fresh out of college in Ethiopia in 2004, started the business in a small workshop on her grandmother's plot employing a handful of neighborhood artisans.

Today SoleRebels is a multi-million dollar business. It is the world's fastest-growing African footwear brand and first to emerge from a developing nation. Its iconic brand is featured in the pages of glossy magazines across the globe.

Through SoleRebels, Tihahun Alemu has created hundreds of well-paid jobs in Ethiopia and she emphasizes that the development of the continent should be achieved by means of *prosperity creation* in which the local people are allowed to make best use of their talents and resources rather than *poverty alleviation* with charity hand-outs.

Tilahun Alemu has of course received numerous awards and accolades. She was, for instance named as one of Africa's Most Successful Women in 2012 and listed on *Forbes* magazine's 20 Youngest Power Women in Africa in 2011. She was also the first female African woman entrepreneur to speak at the Clinton Global Initiative.

Tilahun Alemu talks of an urgent need for African self-sufficiency and the creation of its own world-class brands. She is no great fan of receiving charity and the images of Africa portrayed by most charitable organizations.

She says, "Let's face it. It's pretty hard to convince someone to buy what you are selling when someone else has convinced them that you are solely occupied with swatting flies away from your face."

Perhaps even better known than fashion leaders are those Africans whose music is being heard around the world. Ever heard of Youssou N'Dour, Akon, and Hugh Masekela? Straight out of Africa.

MUSIC MAN MINISTER

Over the years N'Dour gained an extensive worldwide fan base and became one of the most celebrated African musicians of all time. *Rolling Stone* magazine once wrote that in much of Africa he was "perhaps the most famous singer alive." In Senegal he certainly became a highly visible and much loved cultural icon. He is also very active in social issues and in 1985 organized a concert pushing for the release of Nelson Mandela.

As his career developed he opened his own recording studio and then his own record label. He composed an African opera which premiered in France and he wrote and performed the official anthem of the 1998 FIFA World Cup. He was later named Goodwill Ambassador of the United Nations' Food and Agriculture Organization.

Folk Roots magazine described him as the African Artist of the Century. He won his first American Grammy Award (best contemporary world music album) in 2005. He is the proprietor of one of the biggest circulation newspapers in Senegal, a radio station and TV station. As an actor he portrayed abolitionist Olaudah Equiano in the movie *Amazing Grace*.

In 2008 he launched a microfinance organization named Birima and the following year released his song *Wake Up (It's Africa Calling)* to help boost health applications in Africa. His album *Immigrés* transmitted a message to Senegalese expatriates struggling in Europe that they could always return home. N'Dour himself has always kept Dakar as his home base.

Add it all up and you get a man who is a singer, percussionist, songwriter, composer, actor, businessman and politician.

JUST AKON IS ONE OF THE RICHEST

The Senegalese-American simply known as Akon in October 2013 headed *Forbes Africa's* top ten richest African artistes list. The R&B and hip hop sensation first gained international attention in 2004 following the success of *Locked Up* the first single from his debut album *Trouble*. Since then he has launched two hit record labels of his own, Konvict Muzik and Kon Live Distribution. His second album, *Konvicted,* received three nominations for the Grammy Awards in two categories, Best Contemporary R&B Album and Best Rap/Sung Collaboration.

He is the first solo artist to hold both the number one and two spots simultaneously on the *Billboard* Hot 100 charts twice and *Billboard* ranked him number six on their list of Top Digital Songs Artists of the decade. He has had five Grammy Awards nominations and has produced many hits for artists such as Lady Gaga, Colby O'Donis, Kardinal Offishall, Leona Lewis and T-Pain.

Looking ahead, Akon says his goal is to give back to his continent. His first step was to establish Konfidence, a Senegalese foundation that's working to build schools and hospitals in the country.

He says, "I have learned a lot along the way and the person you see today is not the one from yesterday. I am going to keep advancing, doing as much as I can, but I really want to make the biggest impact in Africa."

THE MUSIC OF MASEKELA

Hugh Masekela, legendary trumpeter, jazz innovator, performer, composer, producer and activist. The South African native is a man of many roles.

He began playing at an early age and a major influence for him was anti-apartheid activist Father Trevor Huddleston. Masekela joined the Huddleston Jazz Band, the country's first youth orchestra, and after the 1996 Sharpeville Massacre, with assistance from Huddleston, left South Africa to study in London and New York.

Masekela's music strongly reflects the joys and struggles of his personal life in the brutal white-dominated South Africa regime of the 1950s and 1960s. As an activist, he emotionally vocalized a stand against discrimination and raised worldwide awareness of apartheid with his 1980's hit song *Bring Him Back Home* which became an anthem for the Free Mandela campaign.

In 1986 with other superb South African musicians he collaborated on Paul Simon's album *Graceland*, a ground-breaking partnership that gave international exposure to the sensuous and expressive sounds of "Township Jive."

The year 2010 was a significant one in Masekela's life. He was awarded The Order of Ikhamanga, South Africa's highest civilian honor, and he performed his infectious song *Grazing in the Grass* at the opening ceremony of the World Cup in front of a global television audience of more than half a billion.

Music critics say that Masekela has been a defining force preserving his homeland's musical heritage and a powerful advocate for human rights.

THE MAN WHO PLAYED MANDELA

Nelson Mandela was certainly one of the most inspiring and influential people of the last century, but actor Idris Elba has a special connection. He won a Golden Globe nomination for his portrayal of Nelson Mandela in the film *Mandela: Long Walk to Freedom*. But the role meant more to him than an award nomination.

The movie, he says, not only put him on the map, but it also changed his perspective on life and himself. Now, he says, he wants to "be a little bit more of a beacon for people who don't have a voice. I've done some work with youth but just playing Nelson Mandela has made me want to do a lot more."

Idris Elba, born to a Sierra Leonean father and a Ghanaian mother, began his acting career in the U.K. starring in movies such as *Bramwell*, *Absolutely Fabulous*, *The Ruth Rendell Mysteries* and *Dangerfield*. After moving to New York City, he landed a supporting role on an episode on *Law & Order*, which led to a starring role on the HBO Series, *The Wire*. But it was Elba's leading role performance as a mercurial detective on BBC America's *Luther* that won him the award of Best Actor at the 2012 Golden Globes.

THE WORLD OF WRITING

He's been called the "African literary titan." A "towering man of letters." A "literary and political beacon."

Nigerian author Chinua Achebe who died in 2012, aged 82, was acclaimed for giving an African voice to the stories of a continent that had long been dominated by the writings of Westerners.

He won international acclaim with his first novel *Things Fall Apart* which was published in 1958 when he was just 28-years-old. The book went on to sell more than 10 million copies in 45 languages. It is acknowledged as a classic and became required reading for many students.

Its plot was inspired by Achebe's Igbo family history, a people whose victimization at the hands of British colonial rulers was followed by that of dictators from other ethnic factions. The book was so important that Princeton scholar Kwame Anthony Appiah said, "It would be impossible to say how *Things Fall Apart* influenced African writing. It would be like asking how Shakespeare influenced English writers or Pushkin influenced Russians."

Achebe's writings evolved from a range of influences from harsh criticism of the excesses of colonial power to criticism of African leaders and the people who endured and tolerated violence and corruption. His most vivid work portrays individuals torn between their traditional African values and the invasive Western influence. In his teachings Achebe railed against Western writings about the African continent that he felt, as the *New York Times* put it, "reduced it to an alien, barbaric and frightening land devoid of its own art and culture."

He was especially aggrieved by Joseph Conrad's famous novel *Heart of Darkness* and he thought Conrad "a thoroughgoing racist."

The Nigerian civil war was a calamitous event for Achebe and although he spent much of his later life teaching overseas, his heart remained in Nigeria. Asked about writing a novel set in America his answer was: "America has enough novelists writing about her, and Nigeria too few."

Men of words, men and women of stage and screen, men of music. They all have given us emotional and entertaining portrayals of Africa. They have each contributed in their own unique way to the revolution that is Africa.

Chapter 4. Business and Finance

In Africa today, we recognize that trade and investment, and not aid, are pillars of development.

–PAUL KAGAME, PRESIDENT OF RWANDA

What are some of the names that first spring to mind when you're asked to name billionaires? Bill Gates. Warren Buffet. Steve Jobs. Mark Zuckerberg.

But what about Aliko Dangote? Mike Adenuga? Patrice Motsepe? Folorunsho Alakija? Abdulsamad Rabiu? Most people in the West have not heard of them but they are among the growing group of African billionaires who have emerged in the last few years, and feature on *Forbes* magazine's list of "Africa's Richest."

Top of the latest list, with an estimated fortune of $18.3 billion in 2015, Dangote's wealth almost doubled in one year. About 90 percent of his net worth arises from his shareholding in the publicly traded company, Dangote Cement, which operates in eight African countries and continues to expand. Recently he announced plans to construct new plants in Kenya and Niger after declaring in May 2013 that he would build Africa's largest petroleum refinery—a $9 billion complex in Nigeria.

Born into a wealthy family, Africa's richest man first displayed his business acumen when he was at primary school and sold cartons of sweets to fellow students. He studied business at the Al Azhar University in Cairo before returning to Nigeria to work for his uncle.

In 1977, at the age of 20, a $3,000 loan from his uncle enabled him to launch his own business as a trader in cement. Years later he recalled, "The money was quite a substantial amount then. The loan was supposed to be paid back whenever I was okay—maybe after three or four years. But I paid it back within six months."

BUSINESS WIZARDRY

Dangote credits his maternal grandfather for instilling in him acute business instincts and drive. His grandfather, along with his uncle, took him under his wing after Dangote, at the age of nine, suffered the early loss of his father. It was his grandfather who had given him the name Aliko, which means "The victorious one who defends humanity."

Says Dangote, "As his first grandson, he poured his business wizardry into me. I would not be where I am today without him; a very great man, loving and caring."

Dangote went on to create Dangote Group as a cement company and in the 1980s he diversified and started trading in commodities like flour and sugar. About 15 years later he began procuring pasta, salt, sugar and was soon on his way to the billionaires club. The Dangote Group is now West Africa's largest publicly-traded conglomerate and provides jobs for more than 11,000 employees.

An acknowledged workaholic, Dangote's day starts with prayers at 5:00 a.m. He then spends time at the gym before heading for his Lagos head office. A passionate philanthropist he has donated more than $100 million to numerous causes in the areas of health, education, poverty relief and the arts. As befits a man of his extreme wealth he enjoys a few "indulgences"—a $43 million yacht which he named Mariya, in honor of his mother, and a Bombardier Global Jet Express XRS for which he reportedly paid $45 million as a birthday present to himself.

Dangote values time even more than money. His rationale: "Whoever wastes your time is your enemy. Whoever does not respect your time, does not respect you. Try to make the best of your time because any time lost cannot be regained. To every good businessman, every second counts…do not waste it."

Dangote once said "anyone serious about business should not miss out on Africa" and is determined to set the right example as he intends to invest at least $15 billion in African projects over the next five years. As Africa's urbanization is the fastest in the world, the demand for cement can only increase. So Dangote's future seems set!

Dangote encourages the idea of Africans creating opportunities for themselves through entrepreneurship: "An entrepreneur needs to believe in what they are doing. Foreigners are willing to invest, but they want a lead from local people. They take their cue from locals. If we as Africans are confident in Africa, then so will they be. Everyone is upbeat about Africa, its growth and potential."

It's time, he says, for Nigerian expatriates to do more for their homeland: "Let me tell you this and I want to really emphasize it…nothing is going to help Nigeria like Nigerians bringing back their money. Let us put our heads together and work."

BILLIONAIRES CLUB

Along with Dangote in the billionaires club—although quite a few billion dollars behind—are fellow Nigerians Mike Adenuga, Folorunsho Alakija, and Abdulsamad Rabiu.

Adenuga, nicknamed "The Guru," built his $4.6 billion fortune through oil production and telecommunications. He owns Conoil Producing, a mammoth indigenous oil exploration company, and Globacom, a mobile telecom business which boasts more than 25 million subscribers in Nigeria and the Republic of Benin.

After studying in the United States, Adenuga's first hands-on business experience was running his mother's sawmill business, distributing lace and Coca-Cola. His personal breakthrough came when the Nigerian government granted him hugely profitable construction contracts and his first oil prospecting license.

Oil was also the route for Africa's richest woman, Folorunsho Alakija, to build her $2.5 billion fortune. Her Famfa Oil company owns a good part of the fruitful Agbami oilfield. She reclaimed ownership in 2012 after winning a legal battle with the Nigerian government.

Alakija's fascinating career began in the 1970s as a secretary for a Nigerian merchant bank. She resigned so that she could study fashion design in the U.K. and ultimately launched a fashion label called Supreme Stitches that catered to the rich and famous. The president gave her Famfa Oil company an oil prospecting license which went on to become OML 127, one of Nigeria's most successful oil blocks.

Achieving billionaire status for the first time in 2012 was Abdulsamad Rabiu through the growth of his BUA Group, which principally conducts sugar refining and cement businesses. He also has interests in real estate, steel, port concessions, manufacturing, oil, gas and shipping.

GIVING BACK

In South Africa, Patrice Motsepe, whose wealth is valued at $2.7 billion, is a man of firsts. He's that country's first and only black billionaire and the first African to publicly pledge to sign Bill Gates' and Warren Buffett's Giving Pledge.

Motsepe's mining conglomerate, the publicly-traded African Rainbow Minerals, has interests in platinum, nickel, chrome, iron, manganese, coal, copper and gold.

Born in Soweto, he qualified as a lawyer and became the first black partner at a Johannesburg law firm before starting a contracting business in the mining industry. In 1994 he acquired low-producing gold mine shafts and turned them into an enormous money-making venture.

Giving back to the community, Motsepe donated $1.2 million in 2013 to help get rid of poverty and unemployment in rural areas of Cape Town. His commitment to the Giving Pledge is to give half of the income from assets owned by his family to the Motsepe Family Foundation with an initial $50 million donation within the next five years.

Billionaires like Motsepe and his Nigerian counterparts are obviously the most prominent and visible sign of economies that are booming. But it's not just a handful of remarkable individuals who are reaping the rewards of the transformation of Africa—it's across the board.

"Something extraordinary is happening in Africa," says educational entrepreneur Taddy Blecher, who has twice received the World Economic Forum's Global Leader for Tomorrow Award. In a January 2013 article published by the Skoll World Forum, he writes, "In the wake of enhanced political stability and reduced war in many countries it is clear that a vibrant spirit of entrepreneurship is kicking in with vigor."

Like Dangote, Blecher makes the point that it is most advantageous for the people of Africa to take their future into their own hands. He agrees that the real solution for Africa is creativity, hard work, entrepreneurship and the development of numerous of small businesses. This all means more jobs and more buying power.

Adds Blecher, "Ultimately, it will not be through government, foreign aid or bi-lateral agreements that a nation gets on its feet, but as we say in Zulu – vuk u'zenzele – get up and do it for yourself. Africa has the resources, the land, the people, and hence the possibility to get it right. Entrepreneurship, along with the pre-requisite education and skills levels needed, is going to be the glue that holds it all together."

THE NEXT FRONTIER

Global business consulting company Goldman Sachs agrees that the time to do business in Africa is right now.

In a special report they say that the continent "has a major role to play in resolving the world's commodity, food and labor constraints in the near, medium and long term."

Africa is becoming a major player with increasing exports based on its agricultural, mineral and commodities resources. But the continent's potential, says Goldman Sachs, "is about much more than resources as it evolves and climbs the consumption, urbanization and perhaps industrialization curves."

It goes on to say "Africa is looking more than ever like the next frontier for investment" thanks to predictions that it will have the world's biggest workforce mid-21st century and one in 10 Africans in the global middle class by 2030.

RENEWED SPIRIT

The renewed spirit of entrepreneurship is a reflection of the continents historical past. Francis Chigunta, a lecturer at the University of Zambia, says "Entrepreneurship is not a new thing in Africa. According to historical accounts, Africans were big traders who covered long distances to sell their wares and buy items for exchange and sale in their home areas. However, it is only in recent years that systematic efforts are being made across Africa to promote entrepreneurship as a means of promoting growth and prosperity."

Africans definitely have the right business instincts, agrees Benson Honig, a business professor at Ontario's McMaster University: "Africa is a continent of entrepreneurs. You have no choice. If you need a part, you can't order it from somewhere else. It might take six months or a year to come. So you make it yourself."

WOMEN FIRST

You might find it surprising but women are the backbone of the new economy. According to the World Bank the rate of female entrepreneurship in the African continent is higher than anywhere else in the world and nearly two-thirds of women go to work. Even countries that have come under scathing criticism for abuses of human rights and civil liberties fare well when it comes to equality of the sexes.

Women across Africa have founded every type of business imaginable. Take, for example, Lovin Kobusingya, a 29-year-old mother of two in Uganda who sells more than 1,000 pounds of fish sausages a day. "I always knew I was a businesswoman," she says, "When I was in high school, I used to sell illegal sweets, and I made money. I made a lot of money."

In Nigeria, Adenike Ogunlesi got started selling pajamas out of the trunk of her car. Today, she runs a regional children's clothing empire. In South Africa, Sibongile Sambo set her sights higher—she heads up an exclusive charter-aircraft business, and, in Kenya, Ory Okolloh, just 23, helped launch breakthrough crowdsourcing software that tracks emergency events in real time as they happen. Originally focused on the violence following Kenya's 2008 presidential election it is now used by Google.

Magatte Wade was born in Senegal, and educated in Germany and France. Her entrepreneurial career began in the United States. But it was a return home to Senegal that gave her the idea for an international drinks company. She noticed that cola and other sodas were replacing the traditional hibiscus drinks. Worried that the drinks and the heritage would disappear, she helped launch Adina for Life, a company which sells a variety of beverages based on drinks from around the world. After the company became a multi-million dollar success Magatte left her position as CEO and launched a new business—Tiossano Tribe—which produces high-end beauty products based on traditional Senegalese skincare recipes.

Says Magatte, "I want to transform the perception that people have of Africa. I know that the Senegalese are amazingly creative and entrepreneurial and yet when most people think 'Africa' they think poverty, war, disease, corruption, etc. I am working to create the first successful high-end consumer brand to come out of Africa so that people begin to associate beauty, style and quality with Africa."

ECONOMIC POWERHOUSE

All of the people mentioned so far are but a representative selection of the people who are making it happen in Africa. Together, along with countless others, they are contributing to the revitalized Africa. Another way of appreciating their effort is to see how it translates into hard numbers.

Here's how:

According to the African Economic Outlook, sub-saharan Africa's economic prospects is projected to hit 4.5 percent in 2015 and 5 percent in 2016, outpacing the global average of 3.3 percent in 2015 and 3.8 percent in 2016.

Ian Shapiro writing in *YaleGlobal Online* magazine under the headline "The Promise of Africa" enthusiastically showcased from various sources some examples of the African boom:

- **South Africa, Nigeria, Angola, Ghana and Ethiopia** were singled out by Africa Monitor as high-growth economies to watch. Of the world's fastest growing economies, five of the top 12 and 11 of the top 20 are now in Africa.

- **Rwanda**, best known for the genocidal murder of a million people less than two decades ago, is now peaceful and flourishing, with a 7.8 percent GDP growth rate for 2013 and an announced goal of eliminating dependence on foreign aid. According to the World Bank's 2013 Doing Business report, Rwanda is the world's second most improved nation since 2005.

- **Mozambique's** GDP is likely to surge by a factor of 10 in the coming decade thanks to recent discoveries of vast quantities of natural gas.

- **Zimbabwe** has been the recipient of hedge fund investments to such an extent that David Stevenson was wondering in *Moneyweek* whether it might be "the next emerging market dynamo."

Shapiro is by no means the only journalist to cover the African economic miracle. BBC Africa correspondent Alexis Akwagyiram once reported: "While the U.S. and UK struggle to emerge from prolonged recessions and European nations such as Greece and Spain experience mass unemployment, the International Monetary Fund and the World Bank say countries such as Ghana, Ethiopia, Rwanda and Mozambique are experiencing a boom. Many have ascribed this trend to what they believe are burgeoning middle classes in many nations."

It is a trend that the African Development Bank's (AfDB) chief economist Mthuli Ncube has described the growth as "unstoppable."

WORLD VISITS AFRICA

The benefits of peace and democracy and the strengthening economy have also seen a boost to commerce from the tourism industry. The number of international visitors to the region has grown by over 300 percent since 1990, reaching a high of 33.8 million tourists in 2012, according to the World Bank.

"What has really happened is that post the economic crash in 2008-2009, the rest of the world has really woken up to Africa. There's been such good news coming out of Africa from a GDP growth point of view; better telecommunications; improved security; political stability; and improved airlift. It's really become a sort of new scramble back into Africa," says Andrew McLachlan, Vice President for Africa and Indian Ocean Islands, for Carlson Rezidor, one of the world's largest hotel groups.

If there's one occasion that could be acknowledged as a hallmark of the new Africa it was South Africa's successful hosting of the 2010 FIFA World Cup. Under a global spotlight and following years of international skepticism that the country could stage such an event it went off spectacularly well.

From within the country there was some justified self-congratulation with Archbishop Desmond Tutu describing it as yet another "miracle for the Rainbow Nation" and President Jacob Zuma saying, "The world's view of this continent has been changed. When they think about Africans, they now see competent people capable of getting things done by themselves."

Elsewhere, the world view was neatly summed up by England's *Guardian* newspaper: "History will show that South Africa defied fears of violent chaos to host one of the best-attended World Cups ever. It has put Africa on the global sporting map in a way which seemed unthinkable only six months ago."

The country's Ministry of Sport, in a report, said the World Cup had left an intangible legacy of pride and unity among South Africans and had changed the country's image as undeveloped, crime-ridden and dangerous in the eyes of the rest of the world. Obviously understanding the typical outsider's view of Africa, it confidently joked, "To top it all, we didn't have lions roaming the streets and we did have ATMs."

In the long-term, according to a study by risk analysis and finance company Grant Thornton, South Africa's economy should enjoy a $6 billon boost as a result of the month-long World Cup. But the boost in its image might be even more valuable.

In the chapters to come I will explore further how Africa is, indeed, becoming a brighter shade of black. Africa has its share of exciting entrepreneurs and billionaires. It is building infrastructure to compare anything in the world. It has made dramatic strides improving health and education. Even in the world of high-tech, Africa is a pioneer.

Chapter 5.   Peace and Democracy

Africa has undergone significant changes in the last 50 years.

—UNITED NATIONS REPORT

Bashir Osman is a man with a mission. Some may think he is crazy; foolhardy at best. He may just be an optimist, or he could be a visionary. Osman certainly has a passionate belief in his homeland and a dream that he is determined to make a reality.

Osman's homeland is Somalia, a country that has been more in the headlines for its lawlessness and violence than anything else. Osman is building a luxurious multi-million dollar beach resort in Mogadishu, the country's capital.

"I knew one day that Mogadishu will become peaceful and we'll get stability," he says, "That is why I started to buy that land."

Security is most definitely still an issue in Somalia but in September 2012 after more than 20 years of violence, the East African country picked its first president elected on home soil in decades.

And, just over a year later, on October 26th, 2013 that president, Hassan Sheikh Mohamud, was able to welcome Ambassador Jan Eliasson, Deputy Secretary General of the United Nations, praising the visit as "historic" and the opening of a new UN office as a "vote of confidence in the new Somalia."

Mogadishu has been experiencing an economic renaissance boosted by members of the diaspora returning home to rebuild the country as well as through the efforts of patriotic citizens like Bashir who already owns two hotels in the city and stayed put through all of the violence.

And it's not just notorious hot spots like Mogadishu. Major international hotel groups are building thousands of new rooms all over the continent eager to take advantage of the increasing peacefulness and business growth—especially in capital cities like Johannesburg, Nairobi, Kigali and Lagos.

Hilton Worldwide's senior vice president of development, Patrick Fitzgibbon, explains, "There's a growing demand in those capital cities because they are the centers of business, of government and of commerce—all of which have hospitality needs. We have a very bullish feel for these markets and we are very excited about the opportunity Africa presents. I think that for the next 20 years we are going to have our hands full with opportunity."

Hilton is certainly putting its money where its mouth is. The group has plans to add 5,200 rooms and 17 properties to the 11,000 rooms and 37 properties it currently operates on the continent. Other giant hotel chains are doing the same with plans for 40,000 new rooms in 207 hotels.

AFRICA RISING

It's a far cry from the just a decade or two ago when wars and lawlessness in many African countries made the continent the last place on earth that people would want to visit. International attitudes are beginning to change. The *Economist* magazine is a classic example. In a famous headline in 2000 it labeled Africa as the "Hopeless Continent." By March 2013 it had changed its tune and ran the headline "Africa Rising: A Hopeful Continent."

At this point a little history is in order. In 1945, as World War II came to an end, almost every country in Africa was under colonial rule or administration. By the end of the 1970s most had gained their independence. At the end of the cold war only three countries (out of 53 at the time) had democracies. Today, only a handful of countries don't have a multiparty constitution.

Says *The Economist*, "Armies mostly stay in their barracks. Big-man leaders are becoming rarer, though some authoritarian states survive. And on the whole more democracy has led to better governance: politicians who want to be re-elected need to show results."

In the past decade war and civil strife have declined dramatically. Millions of people are living peaceful lives in countries such as Angola, Chad, Eritrea, Liberia and Sierra Leone, notorious for frequent upsurges of violence. The Arab Spring in north Africa inspired the rest of the continent.

Sierra Leone, for example, has enjoyed a decade of peace after an 11-year civil war that left 50,000 of its citizens dead. Fewer than a hundred people out of a population of seven million are murdered a year—a fifth of the rate in New York. Private guns have been banned and, in a remarkable turnaround, Sierra Leone, once patrolled by blue-helmeted UN troops, contributes soldiers to similar missions in other countries.

What has changed? The cold war "meddling" of the American and Russian superpowers for one thing. Both countries stopped bankrolling their 'own' dictators. UN peacekeeping in Africa, to a large extent with African forces, has become more extensive. And some wars just burned themselves out. After fighting for almost 30 years, for instance, after Angolan guerilla leader Jonas Savimbi was killed in 2002 his army simply gave up. Liberia went through two cycles of bloody civil war ending with the indictment of warlord-president Charles Taylor and his sentencing at the International Criminal Court to 50 years in jail.

Rwanda, even more remarkably, tried 400,000 genocidal killers in *Gacaca* community courts and South Africa, as is well known, pioneered truth and reconciliation commissions.

The power of the people was keenly on display in Senegal when President Abdoulaye Wade—in spite of term limits—tried to run for a third term. The population loudly spoke up in protest and he was depicted in a popular cartoon ordering a third cup of coffee in a bar while removing a sign stating, "Everyone just two cups." More than two dozen opposition candidates joined forces to stand against him. Wade was resoundingly defeated, a defeat which he readily accepted. The capital city of Dakar was the scene of wild celebration—and then everyone went back to work. Democracy had broken out!

Mo Ibrahim, who made a multi-billion dollar fortune developing the mobile communications market in Africa, credits the Internet for easing tensions between ethnic groups. He says, "The more we know about each other, the more difficult it is to sow discord. Through modern communication, Africans will learn that it's better to do business with each other than to hate each other."

COLONIAL RULE

In the history of the human race it was not all that long ago that most of Africa was ruled by colonial powers. In 1884-1885 at the Berlin Conference the United Kingdom, France, Belgium, Spain, Italy, German and Portugal divided up the continent among themselves, creating countries and borders as they saw fit.

Independence for the peoples of Africa was eventually regained, mostly in the 1950s, 1960s and 1970s but with the same borders as those established by the colonial powers—borders which had been created without regard to local cultures and which has always been a source of conflict. The drive for independence of all countries was intensified with the founding of the Organization of African Unity (OAU) on May 25th, 1963.

The primary aims of the OAU were to promote the unity and solidarity of the African states and act as a collective voice for the continent, which was, of course, a vital measure to secure Africa's long-term economic and political future. The OAU was dedicated to the eradication of all forms of colonialism as, when it was established, there were some states that had not yet won their independence and others that were white minority-ruled.

The United Nations Economic Commission for Africa in a special report applauded the continent's achievements, saying, "Africa has undergone significant changes in the last 50 years. By all account her transformation has been nothing short of incredible. The resilience and triumph of her people amidst innumerable obstacles, crises, drawbacks and challenges is laudable and a marvel for the rest of the world."

THE U.N. went on to list changes such as:

"Fewer countries today are in civil conflict compared to those living and enjoying peace and stability.

"Healthcare has improved across the board for men, women and children. Immunizeable diseases like polio have been eradicated in all but two countries while epidemic diseases such as tuberculosis, HIV, and malaria have been brought under control due to access to continually improving health and medical services.

"The continent has also done well in universal primary education ensuring that, more than ever before, millions of her children are in school."

The U.N. extolled other remarkable improvements over the past 50 years such as the status of women. It pointed out that there are several sitting female heads of state, including Ellen Johnson Sirleaf of Liberia and Catherine Samba-Panza of the Central African Republic. Recently ending her term there was also Joyce Banda of Malawi, and that the African Union had adopted a 50 percent gender representation policy. There are also three female Nobel Laureates. There had been notable gains in life expectancy, and greater labor force participation as well as improvement of civil rights, upholding the rule of law and the protection of human rights.

Chapter 6. High-Tech Revolution

It's now easier, technically speaking, to supply a village with Internet access than with clean water.

–MO IBRAHIM, MOBILE COMMUNICATIONS PIONEER

Sometimes it pays to be late! Africa has leapfrogged into the forefront of mobile technology while others have been locked into traditional thinking and old-fashioned systems.

As a latecomer Africa has the benefit of tapping into vast quantities of technological knowledge available worldwide. The continent's leapfrogging into the mobile revolution illustrates the power of "latecomer advantages" and is now the origin of new industries such as mobile money transfer.

The numbers are truly staggering. At last count there were more than 695 million mobile subscribers. Sub-Saharan Africa is the fastest growing market on the planet for mobile phones, laptops and tablets and there are more SIM cards being used than in North America. Based on the fact that almost 50 percent of the continent's population of 900 million is under the age of 15 some experts have confidently predicted that by the year 2050 there will be one billion additional people hooked on their mobile phones. What a market!

Far-sighted entrepreneurs have begun to make their fortunes by pioneering mobile technology—whether developing software, building e-commerce websites, or retailing phones and airtime.

MONEY TRANSFER

One of the most amazing illustrations of the impact of mobile technology is the growth of Kenya's M-Pesa program. This mobile payment and money transfer service ("pesa" means money in Swahili) only began in 2007 but already, over 70 percent of adult Kenyans use it and some reports have declared that as much as a third of the country's GDP passes through the system. In comparison, in the sphere of mobile payments, Europe lags far behind and doesn't have more than a few major cities experimenting with nothing more than payments for parking by phone.

This is a phenomenon that hasn't, in fact, happened anywhere else in the world and has placed Kenya's capital Nairobi at the forefront of Africa's technology race. So much so that Google's executive chairman Eric Schmidt described the city as "a serious tech hub which may become the African leader." One of the continent's most prominent technology incubators, iHub, which has over 10,000 members, is based in the city.

SILICON SAVANNAH

The iHub center was the brainchild of eBay founder Pierre Omidyar who saw the need for an incubator for the IT world. He had a former shopping center reconfigured with low-cost workspaces and internet cafes in 2007. Global firms including Google, IBM, Microsoft and Cisco have taken up residence in nearby offices and Ngong Road where iHub is based has been dubbed "Silicon Savannah".

Kenya is now housing developments of all kinds of mobile technology with projects such as m:lab with partners including Nairobi University. Manager John Kieti says, "Essentially, the mobile phone is going to be huge for us in terms of innovation, much more than the PC was a few years ago."

Kariuki Gathitu, is a 27-year-old software developer who developed an improved mobile payments program called M-Payer, which allows subscribers to pay their bills, receive cash and transfer money with nothing more than a few taps on their phone. He says it can end the "check is in the mail" culture—slow payments that can destroy small African businesses operating with tight margins and no bank credit.

INNOVATIVE INCUBATOR

South Africa, of course, is determined not to be overshadowed and mobile technology is being promoted on a massive scale in that country with the backing of a public-private partnership, the National Virtual Incubator (NVI). It expects to support millions of small businesses by using mobile technology to deliver free training in business methods, support to create their own websites, online coaching, access to financial advice and financing, and a wide array of other critical means of support. With 60 million mobile phones being used by the country's population of 52 million it is an obvious connection point.

In another NVI venture, some 50,000 small businesses quickly built websites for themselves using Google's 'wozaonline' tool and in the first three weeks more than 100,000 people accessed an online business school which awards degrees as high as an MBA. NVI hopes that within five years it will enable one million small businesses to employ at least one million youngsters. They say, "The National Virtual Incubator, amongst many other solutions being developed, will help stimulate the already growing entrepreneurial levels in the country, and we hope to share our learning across the continent."

AFRICA'S BILL GATES

That continent-wide aspiration has already been achieved by a man who began his business career writing software in a bedroom of his parents' home in Ghana at a time when the potential of the computer revolution was not realized by many.

Today, two decades later, Herman Kojo Chinery-Hesse is often called "the Bill Gates of Africa" and runs one of the biggest and most successful software companies in West Africa. His goal is nothing less than igniting an entrepreneurial revolution by spreading e-commerce into the furthest reaches of the continent. Chinery-Hesse has developed everything from online shopping malls to electronic ticketing, digital insurance and even digital security.

Chinery-Hesse was actually born in Ireland, studied in the United States and gained work experience in the United Kingdom. But he decided to return to his parents' homeland to pursue his dream. He says, "I'm African. We need development here and it's Africans who are going to develop Africa. I felt a sense of responsibility; apart from the fact that I thought I'd have a brighter future here."

When he moved to Ghana in 1990, Chinery-Hesse had no money but he had a roof over his head (his parents) and a computer. Along with a friend he created software programs which they began to sell like crazy. So they expanded from the bedroom, to a garage, and then to a real office. His company, SOFTtribe, now provides management services to dozens of companies, including major international brands, and it sells products to tens of thousands of consumers.

Says Chinery-Hesse, who was one of the first to truly take advantage of modern technology, "Our rural populations were in a black hole. You couldn't speak to them. You had to go on a screwed-up road and cross a river and so on but today they all have mobile phones. It's boom time, you can sell them all kinds of things from shoes to cement to building materials…it's made things efficient."

Almost from the beginning Chinery-Hesse and his company decided to create software specifically suited for the African market. But like many start-ups they traveled down a rocky road: "There were times when for six months our company got no checks, and we had to share what little money we had. There were times when we had no money to pay salaries; times when we had debts."

Today, he tells other would-be African entrepreneurs, "There is so much opportunity in Africa, there is so much underdevelopment, there is so much that hasn't been done, that it's not rocket science. If you have the discipline, take the dive."

The influence of Chinery-Hesse can be felt just about everywhere. Shop Africa 53, for instance, a subsidiary of his Black Star Line, is a virtual shopping mall for African products and services. Through it companies market their products online and take payments by way of the mobile phone. Shoppers throughout the world can acquire African designed and manufactured goods directly from the local merchants themselves—everything from food, cookware and appliances, to jewelry, art and clothing.

Another innovation is called Keba-Ekong. It's a re-usable plastic card, a form of electronic pay-as-you-go ticketing for travel, theater and other purchases. Or take "Quickie" a way of obtaining insurance. Then there's Akatura, an efficient payroll system and Hei-Julor!!!, a security program that enables someone whose home is under attack to text an alert and their GPS coordinates to police, neighbors and local radio. Yes, as I said, Chinery Hesse's influence spreads everywhere.

FATHER OF THE INTERNET

If Chinery-Hesse is Africa's answer to Bill Gates, fellow Ghanaian Nii Quaynor has been accurately dubbed "Africa's father of the internet." Chairman of Ghana's information technology agency and a professor at the country's Cape Coast University, Quaynor is recognized as a web pioneer who helped set up some of the continent's first online connections. He was the first African voted onto the board of ICANN, the internet corporation for assigned names and numbers.

Assessing the current state of Africa's online presence, Quaynor, who has also been inducted into the Internet Hall of Fame, says, "The health of the internet in Africa is good; we have good connectivity, at least to major capital cities; we also have good wireless through the mobile companies and other forms of connectivity, so connectivity is becoming less of a barrier, except that we are still working on the affordability side of that connectivity.

"Connectivity is not the problem, now it's shifting to the industry and we need to really build strong industries that will serve the needs of the one billion people in Africa. My hope for Africa in the future is that Africa will own its portion of the internet. Africa should strive to participate on its own terms on the internet, not leave it to chance to be determined."

MOST INFLUENTIAL

Mo Ibrahim, who has been named by *Time* magazine as one of the most influential people of our time, was one of the first mobile phone providers on the African continent. This was in 1998 following a highly successful career with British Telecom. He sold his company, Celtel, seven years later for $3.4 billion after it had spread into 13 countries with 5,000 employees and 24 million users.

Ibrahim had spotted a rare opportunity—mobile communications licenses that cost billions in the U.S. and Europe that could be snapped up for a few million in Africa and they were there for the taking. But the timing was probably right, too, for him as Ibrahim had the benefit of his Sudanese roots and his Western telecommunications experience.

This man alone has probably done more than anyone else to advance Africa's digital revolution.

FROM RICHES TO RAGS TO REAL RICHES

While others were developing business empires creating software, communications and ecommerce sites, Ugandan Patrick Bitature had a different strategy. He is the founder and chairman of Simba Telecom, East Africa's largest retailer of mobile phones (the hardware), who achieved success after a turbulent early life in which he almost lost his life. His father, in fact, when Bitature was just 13, was killed by the infamous Idi Amin regime.

The family had been financially secure. They had drivers and many privileges that he says he took for granted. They owned property, farms, buses and cars. Overnight, following the loss of his father, Bitature was forced to become the family breadwinner and began by trading sugar, clothing and shoes.

They were aided by Father Grimes of Namasagali College who, for several years, took in Bitature and his siblings. The turning point in Bitature's life, he says, came when he was just 14 years old. Instead of sitting down at a dining table the family sat down on a mat, and for the first time there was no sugar for their tea.

Initially his mother, who had borne six children by the age of 30, put on a brave face and insisted they just get used to it. But when his youngest brother started crying for his daddy she broke down, crying hysterically, asking God to come and take them all. That night Bitature got the bus to Nairobi and returned the next day with a suitcase full of sugar—15kg.

Says Bitature, "I got the extra through concerned relatives who realized a 14-year-old had come all the way to Kenya just for sugar. Traveling that far in those days was unheard of. It was like going to Syria today. Communication was hardly there. Crossing the border was scary but no one suspected a young kid to be smuggling sugar in a school suitcase."

When he got back home the supply of so much sugar was cause for wild celebration. Neighbors heard that Bitature had obtained the precious commodity and begged to buy some. He sold them half of his supply, and got four times what it had cost. He was soon on the bus back to Kenya for another suitcase of sugar.

Says Bitature, "I automatically realized that I was no longer a boy. I had become a man. That one act had redefined me."

And so his career began. He started by selling sugar, then shirts, then ladies' dresses, then shoes, then opened a nightclub, moved into foreign exchange, and then mobile phones and airtime.

During another turbulent time in Uganda's history, and while still a young man, Bitature was held captive for seven days and his family feared that he had met the same fate as his father. During imprisonment he saw people being tortured on suspicion of being rebels but through the influence of both President Obote's children, with whom he had studied, and

Father Grimes his release was secured. Today his main business, Simba Telecom, has over 100 modern retail outlets in Uganda, Tanzania and Kenya and employs more than 1,500 people.

SPACE RACE

While the focus on the amazing expansion of mobile technology is obvious to so many Africans on the ground, both in the cities and the countryside, some African countries have less obvious and more far-flung ambitions: they want to reach for the stars. Currently, just a few countries have their own space programs—South Africa, Nigeria, Egypt and Morocco—but rushing to join them are Ghana and Ethiopia. In 2012 Ghana opened its Space Science and Technology Center designed to "foster teaching, learning, and commercial application of space research." It plans a comprehensive space agency by 2016. Ethiopia, meanwhile, has set up two mountaintop telescopes at a cost of $2.5 million.

But what is really gaining traction is the idea of a full-blown African Space Agency called "AfriSpace." An African Union working group on space, chaired by South Africa with representation from Nigeria, Ghana, Kenya, Egypt and Algeria.

The application of space science technology is a critical part of developing the continent and plays a central role in everyday life, for energy, food, security, health, education, environmental management, you name it.

This is another area where Africa is seeking independence. Until now most of the continent's space programs have been partnered with foreign countries. So while it might be expensive to invest in space technology, long term dependence on buying satellite services from elsewhere would be even more cost

SEARCHING THE STARS

South Africa is also taking the lead in space exploration in another way. It is going to be one of two homes (the other is in Australia) for a massive deep space telescope project called the SKA—The Square Kilometre Array. The country's former science and technology minister Naledi Pandor described the project as the largest science-based capital injection Africa has ever seen.

The $2 billion SKA will have a total collecting area of approximately one square kilometer and its size will make it 50 times more sensitive than any other radio instrument on the planet. It will survey the sky more than 10,000 times faster than any telescope ever before. Construction is expected to start in 2016.

There's no doubt that Africa's ability to take full advantage of technology is key to its future. A report from the African Union titled "On the Wings of Innovation: Africa 2024," issues major recommendations concentrating on the need to promote emerging technologies, construct basic infrastructure, invest in higher technical training, and encourage entrepreneurship.

Already there have been infrastructure improvements that are symbolic of the changing face of Africa.

Chapter 7. The Changing Face

We have the blessing of the wealth of our vast resources, the power of our talents and the potentialities of our people. Let us grasp now the opportunities before us and meet the challenge of our survival.

- KWAME NKRUMAH, FIRST PRESIDENT AND FIRST PRIME MINISTER OF GHANA

Satellite pictures taken at night make it appear that Africa is still the "dark continent." From the vantage point of 20,000 miles in space the contrast between the brilliant lights of Europe and America and the seemingly empty blackness of Africa is quite remarkable. You might be forgiven for thinking that the continent is devoid of electricity and is nothing but jungle and wilderness.

But down on the ground it is a different story. A modern, even futuristic, infrastructure is under construction with projects that surpass anything anywhere else in the world.

On the mighty Congo River, for instance, the biggest hydroelectric project in the world is envisaged, twice as large as the current record-holder, the massive Three Gorges Dam in China.

There are plans for multi-billion-dollar high speed rail that will be the envy of the world. There are entire new skyscraper cities being built in many countries that will provide homes for hundreds of thousands of residents. The power of solar and other renewable sources of energy is being harnessed to as great an extent as anywhere on the planet. South Africa alone has allocated $97 billion for infrastructure projects over the next few years.

From water, through land, to rail, and via air, massive developments are taking place. Let's explore some of the continent's infrastructure enhancements in a bit more detail to gather a fuller appreciation of this ever-changing face. Take that hydroelectric project masterminded by the Democratic Republic of Congo, for starters.

The construction of the first phase of a new set of energy projects at the country's Inga Falls is set to start in 2015. The $12 billion development is projected to produce 4,800 megawatts (MW) of power; half is to be sold to South Africa.

Reporting on the announcement in June, 2013 CNN commented, "The world will have seen nothing like it. It is being hailed as the Holy Grail for power; the biggest hydroelectric project ever built that would harness sub-Saharan Africa's greatest river and light up half of the continent."

MIND-BOGGLING CAPACITY

The DRC government's ambitious vision for its "Grand Inga" mega-project involves five additional stages ultimately delivering a mind-boggling capacity of 40,000 MW—double the amount generated by China's Three Gorges dam which is currently the world's largest hydro project. Once finished, Grand Inga could provide more than 500 million people with renewable energy.

It can't come soon enough for the people of the DRC as only a shade over 11 percent of the population currently has access to constant electricity. Until now the power potential from the Congo River's rapids has largely gone unexploited even though its 4,700 kilometers makes it Africa's second longest river, after the Nile, and, in terms of flow, the world's second biggest, after the Amazon.

Elsewhere in Africa other projects are in the works to 'rev up' power capacity. In Ethiopia the stupendous 1.9GW Gilgel Gibe dam/generating complex located on the Blue Nile River is another ray of hope in a once troubled region.

In Chad, the rural power supply system is being largely installed from scratch including a new oil-fuelled plant at Farcha. In South Africa, the first 800MW coal-powered generator at the Medupi Power Station in Limpopo province should be helping the country's struggling grid. Five additional generators are scheduled to open within the following four years.

SOLAR SPECTACULAR

Meanwhile, many African countries are racing ahead of the rest of the world in their use of solar energy.

In 2012, for instance, South Africa enjoyed the world's highest growth in renewable energy investment, from a few hundred million dollars to $5.7 billion, mostly in solar power projects.

The spectacular surge comes as South Africa moves to reduce its dependency on coal, which currently accounts for 86 percent of its energy. To achieve that, the country has set the ambitious target of generating 18 gigawatts (GW) of clean energy by 2030.

The Jasper Power Project, a 96 MW solar photovoltaic (PV) plant in Northern Cape, which has financial backing from Google, will be one of the biggest solar installations in the continent, able to generate power for 30,000 homes.

This project, and others, is desperately needed on a continent whose citizens have the lowest access to electricity in the world and more than half of its countries experience costly power outages on a daily basis. Experts say investments in large-scale solar power projects could transform a continent whose rapidly-growing populations will dramatically increase energy demands.

One of those experts, Frank Wouters, deputy director-general of the International Renewable Energy Agency, says, "Six out of the 10 fastest economies in the world (over the past decade) were in Africa, and that requires much more energy, at a faster-growing pace than we've seen before."

While South Africa is obviously setting the pace, other countries are also striving to take advantage of their natural sunshine. Near the end of 2012, plans were announced to build the 155 MW Nzema Project in Ghana. One of the biggest solar energy plants in the world, the $350 million facility will be fully operational in 2017. In April 2013, Mauritania launched a 15 MW facility designed to deliver 10 percent of the country's energy capacity. A few weeks later construction of a 160 MW concentrated solar power technology plant got under way in Morocco, and so the list goes on.

REVOLUTIONARY RAIL

South Africa is also setting the pace on the transportation forefront with its plans for high-speed rail. Passenger trains zooming through the countryside at 300 km per hour are planned for the trip between Johannesburg and Durban. It's the first phase of an $18 billion rail project, lauded as a new era for South Africa's transportation system, designed to alleviate pressure on overcrowded roads.

When it comes into operation in 2025 each train will carry 600 people over the 600 km journey with a total of round 17,000 passengers a day, rising to more than 33,000 passengers a day by 2050. Freight trains on the same route will move 48 standard containers at 160 kph, shifting up to 4.2 million tons a year. This rail link follows the establishment of the fast Gautrain which is already up and running connecting Johannesburg and Pretoria.

SKYSCRAPER CITIES

Could fast rail one day link major cities across the whole continent, including those new cities that are appearing on the African landscape? Where plains and bush once existed, beautiful cities with manicured lawns and gushing fountains are springing up. They are usually built according to a master plan and located within striking distance of existing metropolises that are struggling to support their teeming masses.

Shining skyscrapers reaching as high as 75 stories towards the heavens—home to luxury condominiums. Five star restaurants. Recreational facilities to rival any in Europe and abroad. Bustling shopping centers boasting premier brand names. Magnificent office blocks where the best minds can do business in comfort. Medical centers with the most modern equipment. Theaters. Broad, brightly-lit avenues. These are the African cities of the future.

One such city is under development outside of the Kenyan capital of Nairobi. Its official name is Konza Techno City, but it is what has earned the label "Africa's Silicon Savannah."

The multi-billion dollar city, situated over 5,000-acres, is the Kenyan government's flagship mega project born with the idea of boosting the country's high tech industry and creating nearly 100,000 jobs by 2030. When completed it will feature a central business district, a university campus, urban parks and residences for 185,000 people.

Also in Kenya, Tatu City is a new decentralized urban center 15 kilometers to the north of Nairobi. This project, on more than 1,000 hectares of land, is being built in 10 phases. The mixed-use satellite city is projected to be completed by 2022 at a cost of over $4 billion and will be home to 77,000 residents.

In Ghana, two mixed-use satellite cities—Appolonia in Greater Accra and King City in Western Ghana—will house more than 160,000 people. All planning and detailed designs have been completed for homes, and retail and commercial centers, as well as schools, healthcare and other social amenities. Basic infrastructure work is about to begin.

Also in Ghana, Hope City is a $10 billion high-tech hub planned to be constructed outside Accra, aiming to turn Ghana into a major information and communications technology player. Designed to house 25,000 residents and create jobs for 50,000 people, it will consist of six towers of different dimensions, including a 75-story, 270 meter-high building that is expected to be the highest in Africa.

RECLAIMING THE LAND

In Lagos, there's an ambitious project under way on 10 square kilometers of land reclaimed from the Atlantic Ocean. Called Eko Atlantic it's a multi-billion dollar residential and business development located on Victoria Island that will deliver upmarket accommodation for 250,000 people and jobs for a further 150,000.

In the Democratic Republic of Congo lies another major reclamation undertaking. La Cite du Fleuve is a luxurious housing project planned for two islands on the Congo River in Kinshasa, which is not only the country's capital but also one of the continent's fastest growing cities. There are plans over the next 10 years to reclaim about 375 hectares of sandbanks and swamps to build thousands of riverside villas, offices and shopping centers.

Rwanda's capital and biggest city, Kigali, is determined not to be left behind and intends to transform itself into the "center of urban excellence in Africa." To that end city leaders have instigated a grand urban development plan—the 2020 Kigali Conceptual Master Plan. It incorporates Singapore-like commercial and shopping areas boasting glass-box skyscrapers and luxurious hotels, as well as leafy parks and entertainment centers.

Also worth mentioning is a large-scale urbanization program under way in Angola, mostly concentrated in Luanda and financed largely by exports of oil to China.

AIR

From land and sea to opening the skies. One of the most ambitious air transportation plans is in Senegal. There, a new $1 billion international airport is being built outside of Dakar as part of the country's far-reaching goal of becoming a serious "gateway contender" for the entire West African region.

So, if you think of Africa as nothing more than jungles, deserts and shanty towns—think again. If you think of Africa has a continent rife with contagious epidemics—think again. The health of the peoples of Africa is also taking a turn for the better as we shall see in the next chapter.

Chapter 8.   Health and Education

Interventions have prevented a large number of deaths.

—JO LINES, MALARIA EXPERT

Statistics tell the revealing story of the dramatic improvements in health and education in Africa. Let's first look at the temperature of the health of the continent. According to a United Nations report released in 2013, Africa has undergone a remarkable change for the better.

LIFE EXPECTANCY

Africans are living longer! Between 1960 and 2010 average life expectancy increased substantially—nearly 15 years. Progress stalled during the 1990s, due to the AIDS epidemic, but recovered during the 2000s. Between the years 1990 and 2010 maternal mortality decreased by 42 percent while the death rate of under-fives decreased by 47 percent.

HIV/AIDS

According to the United Nations, the number of AIDS-related deaths in Sub-Saharan Africa plummeted in just six years; in 2011 it was 33 percent less than the number in 2005. The number of new HIV infections in 2011 was 25 percent less than 2001.

The numbers were just as encouraging on the treatment side: the number of HIV positive people receiving anti-retroviral treatment in 2012 was over seven times the number receiving treatment in 2005, "with nearly 1 million added in the last year alone."

MALARIA

Since 2000 deaths from malaria have dramatically fallen by 49 percent in the general population and 54 percent among children. South Africa hopes to completely eliminate malaria by 2018.

This is all the result of an aggressive campaign on different fronts: widespread use of insecticide-treated nets, indoor spraying and potent malaria medications.

"For the first time we have achieved very large-scale vector control coverage in Africa, and these interventions have prevented a large number of deaths and greatly reduced the burden of transmission," said Jo Lines, a malaria expert with the London School of Hygiene & Tropical Medicine. "So while there is a lot of attention still rightly focused on how we can win the battles of today or next week or next year, we can start turning our attention to the longer-term and think about what is needed to win the war."

Tuberculosis mortality rates, by the way, have also significantly fallen—by almost 40 percent across the continent since 1990.

VALUE OF VACCINATIONS

African countries have made staggering progress in increasing the rates of immunization against measles. By 2010, according to the African Development Bank, 21 countries had measles immunization rates of over 90 percent for one-year-olds.

Immunization coverage for Hepatitis B, diphtheria, tetanus, and pertussis has been massively scaled-up. Immunization for HepB increased from less than 1 percent of one-year-olds in 1990 to 71 percent by 2011. And consider this: the rate of polio vaccination has jumped sensationally. In 1981, only about 5 percent of African children were vaccinated against polio but by 2011 this had risen five-fold to 76 percent.

ZAMBIA LEADS THE WAY

When a country seriously focuses on making the good health of its citizens a top priority, truly wonderful improvements can be accomplished. Take Zambia, for example, where I'm proud to say my father, Dr. Joseph Kasonde, is the Minister of Health and has played a leading role. Zambia's numbers are quite impressive.

- Maternal mortality has declined by 40 percent.

- Malaria deaths have been reduced by 67 percent.

- More than 75 percent of pregnant women with HIV have been given anti-retroviral drugs and counseling to help stop transmission of the disease.

- Contraceptive use has stepped up from 15 percent to 41 percent.

This has all happened in a decade since the Zambian government recognized the importance of primary and reproductive health by dramatically increasing funding by as much as 50 percent. Services are provided free of charge in the public sector and 650 new rural health posts were announced to improve the provision of services.

Referring to the fact that polio has been eliminated and malaria too can be eliminated, Dr. Kasonde says "We have done it before and we can do it again".

In 2012, Minister Kasonde was one of 16 to be named as a Harvard Health Leader as recognition for demonstrating leadership and commitment to strengthening health systems and improving health outcomes. Zambia's commitment to reproductive health is of such significance that it was also awarded the prestigious Resolve Award during the 66th World Health Assembly in Geneva, Switzerland in May 2013. The award recognizes the country's efforts to provide the services to everyone in a convenient, integrated manner.

Dr. Kasonde, who accepted the award on behalf of the government of Zambia, says, "People do not want to go to separate facilities for family planning and for child health. We are working to meet all their needs in one place."

The work of Zambia and other winners can inspire other nations to follow suit, says Joy Phumaphi, chair of the Global Leaders Council for Reproductive Health: "There are many barriers to reproductive health access. It might be that services are too expensive or inconvenient. It might be abusive husbands who do not want their wives to use family planning. But, as the Resolve Award winners have shown, all of these barriers can be overcome."

AN APP A DAY KEEPS THE DOCTOR AWAY

The mobile technology discussed earlier has enabled Africa to leapfrog the landlocked communications infrastructure that exists in the western world—and some of the most startling benefits are being realized in the field of health. Or, as it is now called, M-health.

"Healthcare has always been a huge concern in Africa, especially when doctors and hospitals are far from isolated or remote areas where care is often most needed: M-health is potentially the answer to this," says Dr. Sam Surka, researcher from the Chronic Disease Initiative for Africa (CDIA).

As Idris Ayodeji Bello, co-founder of a health technology and management company called AfyaZima, believes, once you place a mobile phone in someone's hands instead of you going to the hospital, the hospital comes to you.

His young company won the 2012 Dell Technology Award for a low-cost device that monitors and transmits blood pressure information by way of mobile phones. It is called Blood Pressure MCuff. Bello says. "Growing up, they used to tell us an apple a day keeps the doctor away, now it's more like an app a day keeps the doctor away."

AfyaZima—the name originates from a Swahili word for complete health—is also developing a cloud-based service to store the mobile phone health data.

Bello describes himself as an "Afropreneur" whose mission is to empower people to take charge of their own lives: "When you give people access to health education, they will take better care of their health; when you give people access to education, you will see people do even greater things."

REMOTE EXAMS

Mobile technology is also being brought into play to combat the scourge of cervical cancer which kills more than 50,000 women a year in Africa, according to the World Health Organization. The death rate is so high because more than 80 percent of the time women are not diagnosed until late stages of the disease.

In countries such as Tanzania the problem is worse because of an acute shortage of medical experts and quality screening, particularly in rural areas. But now quality examination can take place anywhere. Under the plan nurses are sent into remote areas equipped with cervical screening and treatment tools to take a photograph of the cervix. They transmit images via their smart phones to specialist physicians. The images are immediately reviewed and diagnosis and treatment instructions texted back.

"Early grade cancers will be able to be treated right in the field, right in the rural area," says Dr Karen Yeates, principal investigator of The Kilimanjaro Cervical Screening Project.

In Kenya, a unique M-Health project is under way to motivate parents to have their children vaccinated. Researchers have developed a bar-coded vaccination card which can be redeemed for farm seeds and fertilizer once a child has been vaccinated.

The two-pronged advantage of the program: not only protecting children's health through immunization but also boosting productivity of small farms and improving the incomes of poor households.

Other excellent examples of M-Health are: TxtAlert, a mobile tool that sends automated SMS reminders to patients when they need to take vital medication and mPedigree which allows you to check the authenticity of drugs, counterfeit medicines being a big problem in Africa. All the patient has to do is send the product's verification code, via free text, to a central online registry. An automatic response confirms whether the product is the real deal. Another app enables patients who do not have any airtime available to 'ping' their doctor for a call back.

ONLINE EDUCATION IN OFFLINE WORLD

Idris Ayodeji Bello is not only focusing on health applications, but also has ambitious plans on the education front. A project called YoKwazi is designed to provide learning resources to students and teachers across the continent that they have never been able to obtain.

Until now broadband constraints have meant that many young Africans have not been able to access major online courses that are provided at no charge.

YoKwazi's goal is to launch an offline wireless cloud device (OTGPlaya) in key community areas which hosts online learning programs. The way it works is that the device downloads content just once and then stores it so that people nearby can access it via their wi-fi enabled devices.

"It's about bringing online education to an offline world," says Bello.

RWANDA'S REVOLUTION

It was not too many years ago that children in the tiny east African nation of Rwanda were among the 800,000 innocents slaughtered as the world could only watch. During a few months of madness in 1994 many children were killed and many more fled from the savagery, but for the children of Rwanda today it is a different story. Look into many classrooms and you will find youngsters attentively learning with the aid of laptop computers.

It is the result of a program called One Laptop Per Child (OLPC) which, since its initiation five years ago, has helped provide more than 200,000 green, white and orange laptops to classes in over 200 schools. The schools have wi-fi access and the laptops contain software tailored for the curriculum.

It's all part of Rwanda's Vision 2020 program which has the goal of emulating a knowledge-based economy like that of Singapore. President Paul Kagame sees the IT revolution not only as a way of modernizing the country's economy but also as a way of helping to heal the nation. He says IT will help his people "find jobs, feed their children and regain their dignity."

Over the last four years 3,000km of fiber-optic cables have been laid and in 2013 a $140 million deal was negotiated with Korea Telecom to provide 4G technology throughout Rwanda—one of the largest direct foreign investments in the country.

Of all the challenges Africa faces education remains at the forefront. It is of particular concern as the percentage of young people increases by leaps and bounds. If Africa can harness its potential through its youth there are immense possibilities as we shall see in our concluding chapter.

Chapter 9.   Land of Opportunity

Africa is the continent that is the land of opportunity.

—FORMER U.S. SECRETARY OF STATE, HILLARY CLINTON

Watch out Asia's tigers, Africa's lions are about to take over. Amazingly, 10 of the world's 15 fastest-growing economies in 2010 were from Africa according to the International Monetary Fund.

While most of the world was ravaged by an economic downturn, sub-Saharan Africa's rich supply of minerals and oil helped the continent grow by an average of 5 percent over a six-year period.

The growth prompted this observation from U.S Secretary of State Hillary Clinton while addressing an annual meeting organized by the African Growth and Opportunity Act in

June 2012: "I want all of my fellow American citizens, particularly our business community, to hear this: Africa offers the highest rate of return on foreign direct investment of any developing region in the world."

"We in the United States like to talk about ourselves as the country that is the land of opportunity. It's a point of national pride. Well, in the 21st century, Africa is the continent that is the land of opportunity."

After reading this far I'm sure you will agree with Mrs. Clinton and the people I have featured in this book. Africa is indeed the land of opportunity and what's important is for Africans to lead the way. At the end of the day it is up to members of the African diaspora as well as those who have never left their homes to be in the vanguard.

Instead of turning to corporate chains, humanitarian aid, charities and other top-down methods we should encourage and motivate individuals and communities at the local level to take charge of their financial futures.

This view is shared by many from multi-millionaire entrepreneurs to nonprofit groups, from CEOs to business professors, and from business consulting firms to venture capitalists. Let me share some of their comments with you:

■ Africa's wealthiest man Aliko Dangote: "Everyone is upbeat about Africa, its growth and potential."

■ Mo Ibrahim who catapulted Africa into the digital age through the explosive growth of mobile communications: "Africa is the future. We're finally part of the process."

■ Global business consulting company Goldman Sachs: "Africa is looking more than ever like the next frontier for investment."

■ Marcin Hejka, managing director at Intel Capital, the venture capital division of the chipmaker: "We think that there will be tremendous growth in the technology ecosystem overall across Africa."

■ Rapper and actor Mos Def supporting Ozwald Boateng's Made in Africa Foundation agrees: "It's about self-sufficiency and about how Africa can benefit itself, having benefited so many nations through its natural resources, history, culture and its people. Now it's about a fair exchange and what Africa can do for itself."

■ Oloufounmi Kouchi who runs a nonprofit group Novi Africa: "Human beings want to be independent. That's natural. So why don't we apply that to African countries? The indigenous community doesn't want food and shelter; they want the ability to compete, to be part of something bigger. To be acknowledged as change-makers."

- Joanne Lawrence, who teaches corporate responsibility and social innovation at Hult International Business School in Boston: "We're all optimists. We all see Africa rising."

- Ngozi Okonjo-Iweala, two-term finance minister for Nigeria and former World Bank vice president: "Those who miss the boat now will miss it forever. The best way to help Africans today is to help them stand on their own feet. And the best way to do that is by helping create jobs."

The term favored by many experts is "local ownership." One good example is Heifer International, a global nonprofit group that partners with the poverty-stricken giving them a chance to become self-reliant with gifts of livestock and training. Its system enables people to produce a surplus of crops, for instance, and teaches them how to sell it within their communities.

Pierre Ferrari, CEO of Heifer, says "The value of the wealth-creating value chain is the ability to engage billions of people in the marketplace so they are not dependent on others for food. Once you have that, you start to see trade begin to build, retail, schools, banking and other things start to come about, and it's the beginning of economic lives."

With a growing middle class, there are people in Africa who want to buy things! This is the rise of the African market. Tapping into these emerging markets and helping African businesses do so is a win-win for the foreign investor and for the development of the continent.

MOST OPTIMISTIC

And it's now "easier to do business" in Africa than China or India, says Thomas Barry, founder of global private equity and marketplace securities firm Zephyr Management, adding "Africa represents a prime case where the reality and opportunity are much better than the perception."

Some of the countries showing the most promise might surprise you. Ethiopia and Rwanda, for instance. That may be because, says the *New York Times*, they "have austere, orderly, patriotic, aid-efficient governments that simultaneously spurn charity aid and focus on foreign-direct investment and private enterprise."

One current strong indication of faith in Africa's growth comes from surveys conducted by the Young Presidents' Organization, a not-for-profit, global network of young chief executives. The YPO Global Pulse Confidence Index of CEO sentiment for Africa swelled in the third quarter of 2013 to 65.8, nearly 2 points above where it was the previous quarter and 4.6 points above a year earlier. It meant that Africa was the world's most optimistic region for the fourth quarter in a row.

The YPO survey also found that 80 percent of African CEOs expected turnover to increase by at least 10 percent over the next 12 months, and 58 percent planned to ramp up capital spending. Nearly half (46 percent) indicated they would probably recruit more people in the year ahead. A huge majority (92 percent) forecast that the overall economic conditions affecting their businesses would be the same or better over the ensuing six months. Optimism indeed!

Africa is a continent of growth in every way imaginable. But just consider the population explosion that is under way and the explosion of human talent that will become its most vital resource. Africa, in fact, has the youngest population of any continent with almost 200 million aged between 15 and 24—a number expected to double by 2045. United Nations predictions are that overall population will quadruple over 90 years.

It's "an astonishingly rapid growth," says *The Economist*, "that will make Africa more important than ever." The magazine adds, "And it's not just that there will be four times the workforce, four times the resource burden, and four times as many voters. The rapid growth itself will likely transform political and social dynamics within African countries and thus their relationship with the rest of the world."

The *Washington Post* had a similar take: "It's a big deal because it's a reminder that growth this rapid changes everything. Pause for a moment to consider Asia's boom over the last 50 years—the rise of first Japan, then South Korea, now China and maybe next India—and the degree to which it's already changed the world and will continue to change it.

"Africa is expected to grow even more than Asia. Between 1950 and 2050, Asia's population will have grown by a factor of 3.7, almost quadrupling in just a hundred years. Africa's population, over its own century of growth from 2000 to 2100, will grow by a factor of 5.18—significantly faster than Asia. In demographic terms, it seems, the Asian century could be followed by the African century. That's an amazing thing."

FASTEST-GROWING

A United Nations report in 2013 concluded, "Africa stands as one of the fastest growing emerging economies in the world compared to other continents. Good governance is work in progress that must continually be improved and enforced in all sectors and at all levels—member states, regional economic communities, and the private sector—in order to make the 21st century a truly African one."

"The African century."

"The land of opportunity."

"The future."

"The next frontier."

"Africa rising."

Throughout this book I have endeavored to reveal the brighter shade of black that is Africa today. I passionately believe that Africa is on the rise and will continue to be for years to come. Opportunity is vast. It is beginning to happen. Many of the inspirational people you have encountered in these pages are definitely helping to pave the way, but more needs to be done. Those of us who were part of Africa's "brain drain," part of the diaspora, need to seriously assess what more we can contribute. Those who have always lived in Africa need to consider what more they can do to seize control of their personal destinies. The colonial days are behind us. It is now up to us.

Printed in Great Britain
by Amazon.co.uk, Ltd.,
Marston Gate.